FROM DOG SLEDS TO FLOAT PLANES

ALASKAN ADVENTURES IN MEDICINE

TRUE STORIES OF A WOMAN PHYSICIAN
IN 1950S REMOTE ALASKA

JEAN PERSONS, M.D.

ᴎORTHBOOKS

Eagle River, Alaska

Art Credits: William "Rex" Rexrode, painting of Jean on cover and on page 95

Ann Townsend, page 6

Photo Credits: Personal collection of author

News Article: The Atlanta Journal (now known as Atlanta Journal-Constitution), Atlanta, Georgia, March 21, 1955, p. 99.

Spelling note: In the 1950s, Mt. Edgecumbe, as currently spelled on maps and locator pages was spelled Mt. Edgecomb.

Published by:

꓅ORꓕꓱBOOKS

17050 N. Eagle River Loop Road, # 3
Eagle River, Alaska 99577
www.northbooks.com

Printed in the United States of America

ISBN 978-0-9789766-2-0

Library of Congress Control Number: 2007926225

iv

DEDICATION

To my intrepid and adventuresome husband, Bob Whaley, and to our three daughters, Michele Whaley, Renee Smit, and Tammy Everhart.

They have funded this venture, copied letters and pictures, and given me invaluable help with the computer. Without them and their steadfast support this memoir would never have been written.

Tanana Hospital Fishwheel
Painting by Ann Townsend

Fishwheels are allowed on the rivers of Alaska only for subsistence purposes, and this is a typical one. It consists of two baskets turned by the current of the river, moving very slowly. The salmon are scooped up by the baskets. They then slide down into a waiting container. The fish are collected twice a day, hopefully before the bears get there first.

Contents

FOREWORD

These tales by Dr. Jean Persons, one of Alaska's best known pioneer doctors, will make you laugh and wince at her adventures. They are wonderful stories of how things were in Alaska before the bureaucrats and business took over.

The book shows Jean's compassion and toughness from finding a dead man sitting in her office when she first arrived in Tanana (so he'd fit into a small plane to be flown home) to suturing multiple dog bites on a little girl not expected to survive the attack.

Jean was a petite single woman tackling a job most men would run from. It meant being responsible for villages and their inhabitants scattered over a roadless area larger than Colorado.

By the end of the book you'll wish you'd been there with her, sharing the emergency flights, the sick babies, and the picnics on the tundra.

Shirley Fraser, M.D.
Anchorage,Alaska

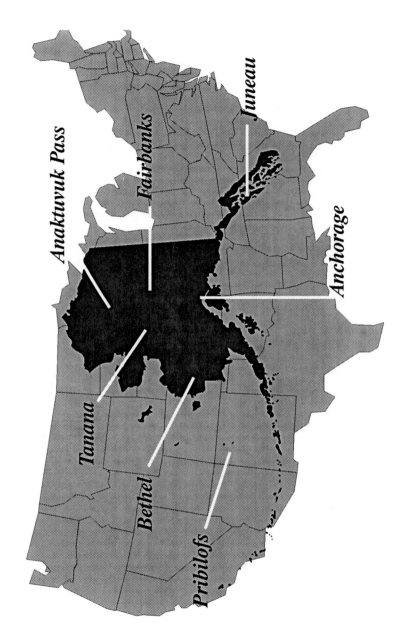

Anaktuvuk Pass

Fairbanks

Juneau

Anchorage

Tanana

Bethel

Pribilofs

HOW BIG IS ALASKA?

PREFACE

The years that I spent in the Interior of Alaska and in the Southwest Kuskokwim area were some of the most rewarding of my life. I have difficulty recalling names of the people, but I have not forgotten them. The stories I have written are mostly from memory as well as from some of the old letters my father and brother Stan saved. There may be some errors as to time and sequence, but I hope my readers will forgive them.

The Natives I cared for were the most stoic people I have ever known. I have the greatest respect for their strength in the face of adversities, such as severe illnesses and the challenges of surviving the harsh winters in the cold and darkness. There was little communication between villages, no electricity other than a few generators in some villages, no running water, and heat only from stoves in the middle of cabins.

It was indeed a privilege to have had the chance to work in the remote areas. I learned much from the people who lived there. The small children were brave, and it was rare to see tears. Despite the outward appearance of little discipline, the children were well behaved, particularly in comparison to some of our non-Native kids.

Medicine has changed amazingly in the past fifty years, and I am sure it will continue to evolve. Back then, as solitary doctor(s) in the small regional BIA hospitals, we tried to give the best possible care to the Natives. We had rare visits from consulting specialists, maybe one a year if we were lucky. We had few support systems and were pretty much on our own.

Nevertheless, we were free to make our own decisions and make changes in the hospital without having to file millions of papers and requisitions or check with our bosses in Juneau or Anchorage. We had no insurance companies dictating what medicines and procedures we should follow. We had no fear of lawsuits hanging over our heads like axes. There were a few lawsuits in the cities, but the beginning of the proliferation of lawsuits occurred in late 1961, when a powerful

California lawyer came to Alaska to try a case, and since then they have increased like rabbits.

Many other doctors have practiced or are now practicing in Bush Alaska. I hope they will write their stories to save a record of the ongoing changes in village life and medical care.

Jean Persons, M.D
Anchorage, Alaska

Jean Persons, M.D.
treating her patients via radio
from the Tanana Hospital, 1953

ACKNOWLEDGMENTS

To so many I owe thanks...

First off, I owe thanks to all my Native patients, Athabaskan Indians and Eskimos in Tanana, all up and down the Yukon River, along the Koyukuk and Tanana Rivers, and north to Anaktuvuk Pass.

To my husband, Bob Whaley and our three daughters, Michele, Renee, and Tammy, and to their husbands, Karl Wilhelmi, Douglas Nelson, and John Everhart, for sparing them to help me.

To Drs. Arndt von Hippel and William Mills, who encouraged me years ago to write of my past.

To Arnold Griese, my old friend from Tanana, who has helped me with my writing.

To Dr. Robert Fraser who was helpful with the history of tuberculosis in Alaska.

To Matt Knutson who spent hours sorting and cataloging my pictures.

To Peggy Ammann who started editing my first stories.

To Tom and Cy Hetherington who gave me all the grim details of Cy's airplane crash.

To Barbara Bernard who led me first to Paula McCarron for early editing, and then to my wonderful publisher and editor wife, Ray Holmsen and Jan Holmsen, who have given me unfailing support and advice. They have made writing a pleasure.

To Bonnie Bell, for the book that she gave me, *Eats, Shoots & Leaves*, in the hopes that it would help my punctuation.

To my writer's group who have borne with me patiently while I read my stories to them: Arne Beltz, Stella Cooley, Marvin Fuhs, Louise Gallop, Dee Heim, Lois Hermansen, Peggy Hicklin, Jan Jones, Jean Matyas, Maxine Rader, and Dorothy Roberts.

Lastly to Dr. Shirley Fraser who so kindly agreed to write the foreword to this book.

To Be a Doctor

In 1945 after two years at Louisiana State University in Baton Rouge, I applied to the Louisiana State University School of Medicine in New Orleans. A number of my friends did not pass the entrance exam, but I was sure that I would and I did. Trying to get a few more hours toward my BS degree, I took two exams for credit. One was in French and the other was in geology. For each I studied the subject for a whole weekend, then took the exam on the following Monday. I did not expect to pass so never bothered to check the exam results and forgot about them.

During my last free summer, I got a job in the local Bastrop, northeast Louisiana hospital. There were two doctors in town. One was a general practitioner, the other a surgeon. The latter, Dr. Don Garnier owned the hospital. I was doing all sorts of work, from working in the lab to being a general handyman. In the operating room I was often a general assistant. One morning a child was having a tonsillectomy. The nurse was giving the ether anesthetic when suddenly a spark flared and the ether flamed. Fortunately someone smothered the flames and, believe it or not, the child had no burns. I was duly instructed never to mention this incident. The child recovered quickly and went home in good shape. Thank goodness.

That fall I entered LSU in Baton Rouge. My father, Frank Persons, wanted me to be a doctor. That had been his great desire and he wanted me to fulfill that wish. Therefore, being obstinate, I refused. But after two months in college, I made the decision to be a doctor. I figured that my work would be to find a cure for cancer to try to make up for my mother's death.

Later I found out how the medical school admissions department worked. The admissions group carefully screened all of the pre-med students who had passed the exams to enter medical school. We were judged not only on our grades, but also on other extra-curricular activities and, believe it or not, on sex, race and religion. There was a quota on girls until World War II came along, and then more girls were admitted. In those days no blacks and only five Jews were allowed per class. No homosexuals then, either. In fact, when we were juniors, one of the boys in our class suddenly was no longer there. Gradually word came out. He was homosexual. There was lots of overt prejudice back then. Fortunately things have improved a good bit since that time. The girls also had to pass a picture test. If the girl was really beautiful she was not considered. The statement was, "She'll just get married." I got in.

That fall my father and Caroline, my stepmother, drove me down to New Orleans from our home in Bastrop, Louisiana. At first I stayed with my Aunt Georgia going to school by streetcar. Soon, however, I found a boardinghouse to stay on Canal Street in the slums. It was close to the medical school and very inexpensive: forty dollars a month for room and two meals a day. Mostly boys, with just a couple of girls. I had nice roommates; one was studying for her Ph.D. in biology. She and I dated two friends. She later married her date. I did not.

Early on we learned about the boarding room reach. We had two long narrow tables for meals with fourteen to sixteen at each table. As soon as the food was placed on the table, most everyone reached for a dish. We had one real obnoxious classmate. He was large, greedy and used the foulest manner of speech. Soon I learned to ignore him, though he had a group of sycophants who followed him everywhere, did his work for him, laughed at his yucky jokes. I could not stand him. I am sure he is dead by now. I shed no tears.

The rest of the group was nice and someone always made sure that I had a chance to get some food.

Anatomy was my favorite subject. There were four students to dissect each body. The bodies were contained in what looked like tin boxes, the odor potent with formaldehyde. First thing we did was to crank open the boxes bringing the body up out of the formalin. Initially we all took a lunch break to eat our sandwiches after carefully washing our hands. After two weeks of taking the lunch breaks we were no longer so fastidious. With a sandwich in one hand, we dissected our corpse with the other.

When it came time for the brain, we took the saw and wore our way with it through the skull so we could open it to study the brain. Alas, our brain had not been preserved properly. Instead, as we opened the skull the brain poured out on the floor looking, though not smelling, like tapioca pudding. For years I could not face tapioca pudding, which had been one of my favorite desserts until then.

2

The physiology professor called me in one day and despite my good premed grades and my high marks on the entrance exams, he told me I would never pass and he would be sure I didn't.

I did not learn a thing in his class after that and ended up taking the year over, this time with a different physiology professor and did pass with no difficulty. Luckily prejudice against women has decreased markedly.

About this time, in 1947, one of my classmates was going up to Baton Rouge where I had gone for my undergraduate years, all two of them. As I mentioned earlier, I had taken two credit exams, French and geology. When my friend went up to Baton Rouge I asked him to check for my grades. Sure enough, I had passed both and all I had to do to get my BS degree was to send the registrar twenty-five dollars. So, four years after I had started the university, I had my BS. Three years later I had my MD from Louisiana State Medical School.

My best grades oddly enough were in surgery. I received a special letter of commendation from Dr. Jimmy Reeves, the head of the surgery department. This was something I've always treasured. Of course, I never went on to become a surgeon because I didn't want to spend four or five more years of residency before I went out on my own.

At that time, we were not allowed on the wards in the hospital until our first two years were completed. Nowadays the ward work starts in the first year of med schools so everything is much more integrated.

One of the more interesting services in our junior year was the psychiatric service. We were instructed not to give advice to the patients. We had just to listen. We were allowed to nod a bit or appear sympathetic, but that was all. That was the time when I learned a lot about life and the words I learned were something else. My education was markedly enhanced. As a clergyman's daughter, I was a bit naive. The sexual habits were another major topic about which I learned a great deal. Later, when I was on the psychiatric service during my general rotation, I learned even more. When we were called at night we had to go into the psychiatric ward with keys to get into the large unit. It was actually like a prison. After unlocking the first gate, I would find a number of the patients sleeping on mats on the floor. These were the calmer patients who realized it was cooler in the outer area of the ward. In those days there was no air conditioning either in the medical school, in Charity Hospital, or anywhere else in the city. This was in the Deep South.

When I passed through these doors on night call, some of the patients in the outer room would awaken and reach out for me. But I would quickly unlock the second gate and slip into the main ward. There was a division between the men's ward and the women's ward. There were two security guards, both large muscular males who would escort me to whichever patient had a problem. After greeting the patient I would go to the nurses' station, which was a glassed in area in the center of the ward. It was kept locked for the safety of the nurses. They let me in so they could tell me what the problem was and give me the chart to review. We were not supposed to order any medication because the residents in the service were trying different medications for the patients. The residents did not want added medications such as sedatives ordered because it would upset their results. This was a problem for us since the residents did not want to be called at night and we were the ones left to face the violent patients. Talking them down was not always easy. One of my friends had her left shoulder dislocated when one of the more violent male patients slammed her against a gate. I was luckier and quicker in dodging contact.

One late night when I was called to the women's ward, I went down and passed through the locked gates with my keys. The two tall, large guards were there to escort me to my patient. But they went only as far as the door of the twenty-bed ward. There they stopped. My patient was a huge angry woman, standing on her bed, swinging a chair. All the other women were out of their beds, crouched in the corners of the room. The nurses were locked in their nurses' station. For some reason it didn't occur to me to be afraid, so I just walked up slowly to her bed, talking gently to her as I went. Glancing back at the guards, I could see they hadn't moved an inch. They seemed frozen. Probably because I didn't look threatening in any way, plus being less than half her size, she began to quiet down and she let me get close to her. She had some minor complaint, which I solved easily. Then she let me order her an injection to help her rest. At this point I didn't care what the resident would say the next day. She got her shot, the other women got back into their beds, and the guards relaxed and then escorted me to the exit.

4

*Jean (2d from right) with other women physicians after graduation
from Louisiana State University Medical School, 1950*

*Jean standing between Mignon Jumel and brother Stan
after completion of internship and one-year Internal Medicine residency
at Charity Hospital in New Orleans, 1952*

In July of 1950 I started my internship at Charity Hospital in New Orleans. We received ten dollars a month with room and board. Charity Hospital was a three thousand-bed hospital, and despite the poor pay was the most sought-after hospital for internship and residency training. The experience with so many and such varied patients was well worth the struggles we had. The only other hospital that might compare in size was the Cook County Hospital in Chicago. The rooms up on the thirteenth floor of Charity Hospital were for the women interns and residents and the fourteenth floor for the male interns and residents. We worked every day and every other night we were on call. We did get one weekend off a month, but as soon as we would get up to our rooms, the phone would ring and down we would go again to the ward or to the emergency room to see whatever patient was in need.

The wards were segregated by sex and by color. Our favorite ward was for the colored women; at that time there was no "black" or "Black American" designation. Patients were either colored or white. Next favored were the colored men, then the white men, lastly the white women. The first were so nice, warm and friendly, that they were a pleasure to work with. The least favored, the white women, were often whiny, complaining, and very hard to please. We all hated to be on duty on the white women's ward.

Each ward consisted of thirty or forty beds in two rows. Drawing white curtains around the bed created privacy. The poor patients, each had one main student doctor in charge, plus one intern, and usually three residents following their care. They all would make rounds every morning along with a professor from LSU or Tulane who was listed as the "visiting man" on our schedules. With the extra interns and medical students, there could be a group of about twenty in total. Looking back, I wonder how the patients could stand seeing us all. The student would present the case with the history, physical, all the lab work, and any X-rays. The intern would add comments, and then there would be a discussion of the "case" with the intern answering the majority of questions. Some of the patients had had many admissions and could prompt the student or intern when they seemed at a loss to answer.

Once as I was coming back from an evening with my date, a classmate met us as we entered the front hospital entrance. He rushed up to tell us we must go to the morgue. Down to the basement we went and there was a newborn with two heads. The mother had had no prenatal care and been admitted in full labor with the baby's head crowning. When the intern, and then the residents who were called, were unable to deliver the baby, they called the visiting doctor. The x-ray showed the problem and the resident alerted surgery. When the visiting doctor came, the need for a caesarian was obvious. However, the time delay was too much and the baby expired. I thought this might have been for the best, thinking that the baby would have probably ended up in a freak show in a circus had it lived.

As interns, on our regular working schedule, we often slipped away for some fun. But that didn't last long because we would often get called back. On obstetrics (OB) we worked ten-hour days for two weeks and fourteen hours at night for the next two. We slept on guerneys on the twelfth floor in front of the elevators. That way as the doors of one of the four elevators opened, the elevator man would call one of the three services, Tulane, LSU, or Independent. One of us would roll off the guerney to go take care of the lady about to deliver. I chose the Independent service as an intern because then we would have consultants from both LSU and Tulane. Tulane was the Medical School I had wanted to go to, but had no money. This way, I got a bit of Tulane.

More than half of the patients who arrived in active labor had never had a prenatal visit. We would roll the patient right into the prep area to be cleaned up for delivery. Some had to go right into the delivery room with the time so imminent. Lots and lots of squalling, "Lordy, Lordy, never again." We often threatened to make recordings, but never did. Then after the baby was delivered the mother, in most of the cases, would tell us interns to name the baby. "You name him (or her), doctor. I got so many at home I've run out of names." We were terrible, naming the poor babies perfectly awful medical names, like leucorrhea or leishmaniasis. I hope the office personnel preparing the birth certificates changed the names.

The service I enjoyed the most was the Emergency Department. Here again we worked either fourteen-hour nights or ten-hour days. It was always exciting. Fractures, heart attacks, diabetic comas, gun-shot wounds, stabbings, burns, and on and on.

At that time we got to ride the ambulance too. My first case still sticks in my mind. I rode up front with the ambulance driver. We rarely had any idea what we were called for. Since I was small and skinny, the burly driver always got out and carried my bag. There was a crowd on the sidewalk in front of the house when we stopped. The driver, carrying my bag, parted the way through the crowd for me. "Make way for the doctor! Make way for the doctor!" I felt a little insecure but walked with my head held high, trying to look concerned and competent at the same time.

In the house someone directed me to a patient in the back room. I walked down the long dark hall, looking into each room till the very last room was reached. It was on my left. Opening the door to look in, I saw a neatly made bed. There wasn't anyone in it. Then I saw something behind the door in a chair, all covered with a sheet. I looked under the sheet to find a male body sitting wrapped in a blanket with no sign of life. His skin was cold. Quickly I pulled out my stethoscope to listen for a heart beat. I was sure I could hear one, but it was obvious that rigor mortis had already set in. I was so disappointed. My first ambulance patient dead. All I could do was to write up the papers for his death certificate.

Others were much more interesting. One call to the French Quarter on a Saturday night ended up with a gun-shot victim. We had to lie down behind the ambulance because the shooter was still shooting from the rooftop across the street. The driver and I managed to drag the poor victim to a safer spot while the police surrounded us. Then we were able to get him into the ambulance and make a fast trip back to Charity Hospital.

Another call brought us to a three hundred-pound man lying on the sidewalk convulsing. It took four men from the crowd along with the driver to hold him down long enough for me to get an injection into him to stop the seizures. Somehow in New Orleans there were always crowds wherever we went. Some in the crowd were helpful, others fainted, and others were just a nuisance.

Once I got to go to the city prison. Carrying my bag, I followed the guard who would unlock one metal gate, bang it closed behind me, lock it, then go through to another, then another till we reached an open area where a big man lay without a stitch of clothes stretched out face up on the floor. A dozen prisoners stood around him in a circle.

8

The guard offered neither information nor help. I checked my patient carefully, but I could hear no heart beat and his skin was beginning to cool. I reached into my bag to get a syringe with a long needle. I used this to pull up some adrenalin, wiped his left anterior chest with alcohol, then plunged the needle into his heart and injected the adrenalin. One prisoner watching dropped to the floor in a faint. My prisoner did not react at all. He was dead. So much for my prison service.

The other prisoners were very courteous as I covered the dead man with a nearby sheet and left, with the guard unlocking and locking gates behind me. Their clang seemed louder than when we had come in.

The ambulance drivers loved to drive fast. One time I had been down to the center of town to pick up a heart-attack patient. After giving him a brief exam and some medication, we were able to get him into the ambulance quickly. I had him on oxygen and I was using suction to keep him from aspirating. Going up Canal Street, New Orleans' main street, was an adventure in itself. The policemen waved us through all the red lights, the driver hitting ninety miles an hour in his attempt to get to the hospital as quickly as possible. As he made his turn off Canal Street, the oxygen machine and the suction machine almost tipped over. Fortunately, my poor patient was semi-conscious and did not seem to notice. I managed with one hand to keep the machines from falling over, but it was very close. The man was admitted quickly. When I went to see him later he was sitting up in bed in no distress and smiling.

The race-car driving by the ambulance drivers came to a halt shortly thereafter when one of them drove the ambulance at such a top speed that when he reached the back hospital entrance, he ran up and over a little red sports car which had just pulled in with a patient with appendicitis. No one was injured, but from that time on the drivers could no longer exceed the speed limit.

As interns in the emergency room, when our white skirts or pants were covered with patients' blood, we would add an apron, wash our hands, and change gloves between patients. Thus we worked until we got off duty in these clothes. Hospitals now would freak out at all the blood and body fluids we were awash in most of the time. Most of us seemed to thrive, despite the contact that we had with all the infectious diseases as well. None of us gained weight with the lack of sleep, over work, and lousy hospital food.

One late-night case stands out most in my memory of the emergency rooms. About midnight, I was in one of the small exam rooms suturing up the head of a nice colored woman. She told me her story between moaning and wailing for her children. It seems that her husband had taken an axe to her head trying to kill her but she had escaped. The x-ray showed that the skull was intact, but blood was copious, since the scalp has innumerable small blood vessels. Blood had been typed and matched. I was trying to get her scalp back together, trying to reassure her that she would be okay. She just kept crying, yet when asked, said she had no pain. Just, "My children, my children." As I worked on her, the story came out. Her husband had come home drunk, shouting and cursing. He had proceeded to pour gasoline over her sleeping children. Then he lit a match and everything went up in flames. She ran to try to rescue them but he grabbed an axe and chased her until he got her. With one blow he laid her scalp wide open. She passed out and remembered nothing but the picture of the flames on her children.

Then the rear hospital door opened and one by one the stretchers rolled in with one child after another burned so badly that if they were not dead on arrival they were within a few minutes. All were so terribly burned it was painful just to look at them.

The emergency room back door opened one more time. Through it was wheeled her husband, burned almost to a crisp but still alive. The specialists came to take care of him. He was taken to a single room on the second floor where a policeman was stationed outside of his door, as though he could possibly escape! I went to see him one time. Not once did this man have any pain. He died on the eighth day and I was glad. I resented the fact that he did not suffer.

One good thing did result from this terrible tragedy. The seven-year-old daughter had heard all the noise and shouting when her father came home. When she saw him coming toward her with the gasoline can she went through her open bedroom window and ran to the neighbor's house. By that time her house was going up in flames but she had not been hurt. To see her mother's face when she saw her one little girl safe and whole was like witnessing a miracle.

10

We dealt with many problems but some were more difficult than others. Patients came from the whole state of Louisiana, since Charity Hospital was the only charity hospital in the state. We had to deal with comatose patients who would be rolled into the admitting area with a note pinned to their clothes from the referring doctor, "Please admit and oblige." No history, no record of medications or anything, just, "Please admit and oblige." Often there was not even a doctor's signature or it was scribbled so illegibly that it was unreadable.

Every year when I was in medical school in New Orleans, one of the highlights of the year was the Mardi Gras celebration. Classes were cancelled, which was just as well, since no one would have attended them.

By ten in the morning on Shrove Tuesday, the last day before Lent started, in this highly Catholic city, a group from my boarding house started walking down Canal Street where most of the festivities were going on. Later on, everyone would move down into the French Quarter where fun activities went on until the wee hours in the morning. Bands played all day long, each one trying to outdo the others as they marched before and in back of the floats. The jazzed up funeral march always sounded the best to me.

The floats were magnificent, the crowds enormous, and all sorts of noises accompanied the many groups singing and dancing in the streets. Firecrackers constantly popped off, adding to the fun. From the floats, candy and favors were thrown, and the kids in particular scrambled to catch them. Many of the onlookers were dressed and partially dressed in a variety of costumes, some extremely eye-catching.

Before leaving the house, we had left any valuables that we had and carried only the money that we might need in our deepest pockets, because the pickpocketers had a field day every year during the holiday.

We had not walked very far before we were submerged in the thousands of people who had come to enjoy the festivities. Soon we were surrounded, literally, packed in the crowd so thickly, that it seemed that we all had to breathe in at the same time and breathe out in a similar fashion. We were slowly propelled down Canal Street, as if we were one single mammoth body.

Suddenly there was a shriek and right in front of our small cluster of medical students there was a flash of knives. Two muscular young men had pulled knives out of their pockets and they began slashing one another. Despite my belief that we could not come any closer to one another, everyone pushed back so that there was an empty circle in front of us except for the two men. The crowd held its breath. There was not a sound save for the grunts from the two fighters and the noise of ripping clothes. Blood was everywhere, pouring from their wounds. Then, before one killed the other, the police were there. How they maneuvered their way through all the people, I don't know. Handcuffs were put on and the young men were dragged away to a blaring police car not far from where we stood, dumbfounded at what we had just witnessed.

Then the crowd continued down the street, breathing as one again. It wasn't until way late in the night that we returned home, tired but happy.

There were so many other happenings during my year of internship. At the end of June 1951, I decided that I did not know enough to go out into the world so I took a year of Internal Medicine residency on the Independent Service. After that I found an opening with the Bureau of Indian Affairs working with the Navajo Indians in Crown Point, New Mexico which is the subject of my next chapter.

Recently, as I viewed the August, 2005 disaster of Hurricane Katrina in New Orleans, I wondered about the fate of patients in Charity Hospital. I could empathize with the doctors' dilemma as they tried to save patients while the waters rose, knowing they couldn't save the patients or arrange for their safe transfer. The doctors themselves were in danger of drowning as they stayed with their patients.

Charity Hospital, such a large part of my life, is gone forever.

CROWN POINT

A Good Training Ground for Alaska

In 1952, when my one year of residency at Charity Hospital in New Orleans was completed, I felt that I was ready to go out into the world. My good friend Beba Kurth, who had been my intern when I was a resident at Charity Hospital, had talked about her plan to go west with the Indians so much, that I thought this might prove very interesting.

I applied to the Bureau of Indian Affairs commonly known as BIA. Immediately I received an acceptance letter with a jillion forms to be filled out. They offered me a place in a hospital in Crown Point, New Mexico, with the Navajo Indians. I accepted for a six-month period, not wanting to commit myself for a longer because I did not know where I really wanted to practice.

My father, who had always longed to be a doctor, would have preferred that I practice in Alabama where he now lived. But, though I loved my father, I knew practicing near him would be a disaster. He would have brought in every derelict in the area to be treated by his daughter. Thus I chose to go west. New Mexico was close enough to him, but not too close.

Both my father and my brother Stan drove me to my new home in the west. Our car was old and rickety, and with all my belongings packed in with great care by Stan, the bottom of the car hung very low. Still, it did make the trip with only half a dozen flat tires.

Crown Point was thirty miles north of Gallup on a narrow road that followed a small winding river. Later we learned that several doctors assigned to the Crown Point Hospital had driven that road, but by going too fast around the curves had ended up in the river, not surviving the trip. We drove slowly and with care.

The hospital was a thirty-bed hospital with ample nursing staff and one other doctor. Dr. Hubert Swartout, a very knowledgeable and helpful man, was the Medical Officer in Charge usually referred to as the M.O.C. He was a Seventh Day Adventist but never pushed his beliefs on anyone. He just lived a good life. I was lucky to be able to start my work after Charity Hospital with him as my boss.

Jean and Stan in front of Jean's house in Crown Point, New Mexico, 1952

Great fun was had by the Indian boys who would turn road signs in opposite directions to confuse new drivers in the wide open spaces of the reservation.

Wagon train procession with Navajo Indians leaving Gallup, New Mexico, heading for Crown Point hospital.

The head nurse was a different matter. I was told that the first thing she said when she saw me was that at the hospital they did not need a high-school kid. She resented me from the very beginning. And I her. She was a pain, but fortunately left a couple of months after my arrival.

The nursing staff was diverse. We had seven nurses. One was a Sioux, one a Zuni, two were Navajo and three were white. Except for the head nurse, all worked together and the patients loved them.

Whoever designed the hospital back in Washington D.C. must have had a medical problem, because each office and every exam room had a bathroom attached, including the waiting room and the hospital lounge. I had never seen so many bathrooms in all my life. These did not include the numerous ones for the patients.

In the basement was the pathology lab where we did our autopsies; the worst of these was on an eight year old who had drowned about a week before. At that time, there was no air conditioning and the summer days were very hot in New Mexico.

My one-story government-style house was about half a block down the hill from the hospital. It had three good-size bedrooms and a moderate-size living room with a beautiful fireplace made of petrified wood. A nice kitchen completed the inside, along with a good bathroom that worked. A phone hung on the wall, which must have dated back fifty years. It was, however, usable with a lot of patience. The grass outside was sparse. I could almost hand cut the few blades. The desert dust was fierce, coming through the cracks in the closed windows. Each evening there would be at least an inch of the red dust on the windowsills, but in my mind, this was a minor problem.

Before I left Charity Hospital, I told all my friends to come visit me, expecting one or two would do so. In the first three months I had fifty-two visitors. This was great except for one family who came with four small children, two cats and a dog who had recently had puppies, and the puppies all came too. I didn't have much money then, just the small amount the government then paid the doctors. I probably cleared about six hundred dollars a month, which was certainly better than my ten dollars a month as an intern and twenty- five as a first-year Internal Medicine resident at Charity Hospital. Still, feeding this family grew quite expensive as well as all the work cooking and cleaning up after them, until, toward the end of their week- long visit I stayed up at the hospital most of the time, letting them do a little fending for themselves. I think that the deciding point to end their visit was when their little two-year-old boy came up to me, and bit me on the thigh. "Oh," said the mother, "That means he likes you." It was a good day when they left on their way to live in Hawaii.

My other friends were all fun and they helped every way they could. One of my visitors was a doctor who came out with his aunt from California. The aunt told me he had come to ask me to marry him, but then he got cold feet and could not brave the question until later when he wrote to me with his proposal. To this question, I wrote a soft, but definite refusal.

Dr. Swartout and I worked every day and took call every other night. It was a great relief to him since he had had to be on duty the whole time before I came. He had a nice family with his wife and, as I recall, four children. When he and his wife went on a trip, I took care of the kids who were real sweeties. As they were Seventh Day Adventists, I had to be careful about feeding them pork, coffee, and soda, anything with caffeine.

We had two drivers for the hospital who would drive out on the Navajo reservation to pick up patients when someone called in for them, as well as to take them home when well. No one had a phone in the hogans, so the general store was the place where calls were placed. Getting the patients in was not a big problem, but returning the patients to their homes was a lot more difficult, particularly if the patient was a child.

The parents in the summertime often worked in a variety of areas, mostly in the carrot fields. As soon as the fields were picked, the overseers moved them to another field. The parents did not have access to a telephone so could not call us with their change of location. They lived in shacks, which must have been unbearably hot in the daytime, earning the absolute minimal wage. Their living conditions were lousy. Clean water and the sewage problems were as poor as could be. Infectious diarrhea was rampant and little children would die of dehydration if they did not get to the hospital in time. At any rate, when the child was ready to go home the driver would go from one of these camps to another looking for the parents. Frequently, the driver was unable to locate the family, so would bring the kids back to the hospital, and then try to find the parents another day.

We had rattlesnakes on the reservation. Since Crown Point is a mile high, the days were hot, but the nights were quite cool. The snakes would come out to sun themselves during the day. On the straggly path, I walked each morning, noon, and evening going up to and down from the hospital, I found a nest of baby rattlesnakes. The mother was never in evidence. Each day I would carefully step over the babies so I wouldn't disturb them. They didn't bother me and I didn't bother them. One day there was not even one there. They had all gone out on their own.

The only time I ever killed a snake was the day that I looked out the hospital window to see some children of the hospital employees playing with a snake. I couldn't see if it were a rattlesnake or not. I raced outside, grabbing a hoe on the way, and as soon as I reached the children did the poor snake in with my hoe. Much to my discomfort and theirs the snake turned out to be one of the harmless garter snakes. I felt very guilty.

The only rattlesnake bite cases that we had during my time at the hospital were with two retarded, now called mentally-challenged boys, ages eight and nine. Each had bent over to pick the snake up and each one came in with bite marks on his thumb. Fortunately, they were able to give an accurate description of the snake. Given anti-venom, they did well and hopefully learned a lesson.

The Navajos lived in hogans, small buildings with the doorway placed in a certain position because of the spirit world. The people were friendly but reserved because of all the troubles the white man had brought them, including having their lands taken away from them. They still used covered wagons for travel and often brought their sick ones to the hospital in the wagons.

One day, I looked out of the hospital to see that there were five of these covered wagons at the edge of the hospital grounds. I wished that I had had a camera then. Slowly they came to trust us. Before I left Crown Point, we had five Medicine Men in the hospital. I took the ones who were able to walk to the clinic area and showed them how to use my stethoscope and otoscope. In turn, they showed me how they did some of their sand paintings.

Early on, no matter how agreeable my outpatients seemed to be with the medications I ordered for their ailments, I found that they tossed them under a bridge that was close by the hospital. Thereafter, if an antibiotic was needed I gave it as a shot. At least that could not be discarded.

In midsummer we had a wonderful dentist, Dr. Anderson, come to the hospital from California. He spent a month with us doing as much dental work as he could in that time. He had a way with the kids. He gathered them together, placing their chairs in a circle, with the dental chair with his needed equipment in the middle. The children sat silently as he began his work, first one child, and then another. He began telling stories and singing. The children were spellbound.

He moved one child after another into the dental chair, did the necessary work, and so continued until each child had been cared for. It was unbelievable to see the dental repairs done without a single complaint or a crying child. One after another was checked and treated, mesmerized by this man. Before they or I knew it, the afternoon was over and all of the children left happily. This was repeated each day, until all the kids in the area had been in for care. The dentist never ceased to amaze me.

My former roommate, Mignon Jumel, from my days in Charity Hospital, came for a visit while the dentist was there. The dentist suggested we go to a Yebechai dance. This was a dance that was being held for a little girl to drive out the evil spirits in her. It lasted for seven to nine days, starting with sand paintings in a hogan built especially for the dance. Out of nowhere hundreds to a thousand Indians gathered from near and far, more and more appearing every night.

For three nights, we looked for the dance, starting out at midnight and wandering over the lonely wagon trails. We went in the dentist's jeep because the area we covered no ordinary car could go. Down into washouts, over the desert where there were no trails, driving without lights so we could see the light of the fires.

On the third night, we found the place. Twenty to thirty campfires with flames flickering brightly and Indians as far as I could see. We left the jeep and walked down into the midst of them, wrapped in blankets because it was a cold night. We walked slowly, because we were the white intruders.

18

As we approached, we saw that there was a large semicircle with a hogan at one end and covered wagons completing the circle. Some of the Indians were sitting inside the covered wagons with their blankets around them and all the babies tied securely on their cradle-boards.

From within the hogan there came a chanting in the Navajo tongue and then the old Medicine Men spoke. All became very quiet, not a single baby making a noise, while everyone listened intently.

Then the dancing started, with some of the Indians making a peculiar "coo," followed by a few shrill cries. All the dancers were masked, two of whom were clowns. These could and did make fun of many things and some of the Indians smiled.

In the distance, we could hear the throbbing of drums, and we three sat a little closer to each other, for we were sitting in the midst of them all.

Suddenly a young Navajo approached us. "White man smoke peace pipe?" he asked. In his hand was a tiny pipe, and he was making a joke. We laughed and the dentist assured him that we would. I was glad he knew what to do, because one never knew what might happen. The pinion fires burned and the smoke became so dense that our eyes burned and it was hard to see. On and on the dances went, the chanting, and the drums beating, increasing in intensity all the time.

Reluctantly we left, but only because the wildness was becoming so great that our dentist friend knew that soon we would not be safe.

The jeep stuck in the sand as we left, but we finally got it through. The coyotes howled. Soon we were happy to be back in our beds. It was hard to believe we were really in the USA.

After my six months at the hospital were up, I agreed to stay for three months more because the BIA had been unable to get a replacement for me. A good thing happened that helped me make the decision to stay a little longer. That was when my uncle in Alabama was able to get a Plymouth for me with the six hundred dollars I had saved up. He had someone drive it out to Crown Point for me, thus giving me a lot of freedom that I had not had before.

On my free weekends after I got my car, I made excursions over the Indian reservation. The desert roads were mostly nothing more than wagon-wheel tracks. It was easy to get lost. In addition, where there were markers on the trails, the little Indian boys thought it great fun to turn the markers in the wrong direction.

I always managed to find my way home, but just in case I might not, I carried a bunch of supplies in my trunk. Dried food, several gallons of water, matches, juices, canned food with a can opener, as well as potatoe sacks that were good to put under the wheel for traction if my car got stuck in the ever-blowing sand. Also, I packed three flashlights, a shovel, and a couple of blankets for the cold nights. Nothing like being prepared.

Before I left the Navajos, I spent a weekend with my friend Beba, who was running a BIA Indian hospital for the Hopi Indians in Tuba City in the Northeastern corner of Arizona. Because my hospital was in the Northwest corner of New Mexico, we were not terribly far apart. One weekend we decided to meet at the airport in Flagstaff, Arizona, and make a trip to Phoenix, Arizona.

It was a beautiful sunny day in Crown Point. I had tanked up with gas in Gallop on the way, and laughed when the attendant told me that we were in for bad weather. The sky was still just as blue as could be. However, shortly after I started again, the sky became really black, and soon it began to rain.

Twenty miles from the Flagstaff airfield, which was a very tiny one way back then, the rain turned to snow. The tiny airfield appeared deserted, however, there was an agent inside, who told us that the plane for Phoenix was due in within the hour. We were the only passengers to board. I think the agent closed the field down after we left. He did not tell us of the major storm coming in, so we had no concern about our return trip. The plane took off with no difficulty and we had a smooth ride all the way to Phoenix.

As soon as we reached Phoenix, we headed for a hotel and after getting checked in, we went out for lunch. Everything was cheap back then. We had steak for lunch, dinner, and breakfast, along with lots of other good things, including desserts. After filling ourselves until we could barely move, we took off on a shopping trip, which was eminently successful. Beba got all the things she needed and wanted. I, in turn, found a wonderful lamp with a shade made of some sort of skin with native animal drawings on it for my brother, a heavy tweed winter coat that I never wore because it was so heavy, and multiple other smaller

20

gifts for my family in Alabama. One big mistake I made, was to wear very high heels, and when my legs gave out, we headed back to the hotel. We ate a tremendous dinner and then went to our room and to bed, with more shopping the next day. About four in the afternoon the next day, we caught a cab out to the airfield to catch our flight back to Flagstaff. We boarded happily with all our gear.

It was a short flight, that is, it was supposed to be. Within fifteen minutes, the pilot announced that the snowstorm had increased to such a degree, that he would not be able to land in Flagstaff but we could get off at Winslow, the next city. Hard to believe, when we had just been in warm, sunny Phoenix. Nothing could we do, so we got off, when the plane landed in Winslow. It had become cold and ice was forming on the wings as we landed.

We collected all of our belongings and got off the plane. Neither of us had any money left other than some small change. Credit cards were not in existence in those days and we knew no one in Winslow. We never asked the airline for help, never thought of that, and probably would not have received any if we had.

So, we set out on foot. It was cold and the streets were muddy. Beba decided that we had better hitchhike. She and her husband Paul had done a lot of hitchhiking early in their marriage, so I agreed. We stood on the corner of one of the lighted streets where there was a lot of slushy snow. I held my beautiful lamp in my right hand, my heavy coat over my left arm while Beba piled all the rest of our purchases by my feet. Then, with her thumb up, she stopped any number of cars. She interviewed the driver of each vehicle that stopped, dismissing the majority. Most of the male drivers did not pass her qualifications.

Finally a nice looking young soldier stopped. He passed Beba's inspection, and he was headed for Flagstaff. He helped us pile everything into his car and we were on our way.

It was a long ride. As we got closer to Flagstaff the snow came down heavily, swirling and blowing around us, making visibility poor and driving extremely difficult. At last we reached the Flagstaff airfield. It was dark and the airport was closed. Our cars looked like giant marshmallows, all covered by eighteen inches of soft, white snow.

The soldier offered to help us dig out, but we thanked him mightily for all he had done, and told him we could take care of everything. He was so nice, but so tired, I'm sure he was relieved with our refusal. He drove off and Beba and I knocked off enough snow so that we could retrieve our shovels from the trunks of the cars.

We worked and worked, finally uncovering the cars, then digging a path clear enough to reach the road. We both were still wearing skirts, as we had in Phoenix, but this did not bother us. We were so hot from all our work but relieved to see the end of our digging.

As we started our cars, the first thing we found was that Beba had a flat tire. We were deflated, but we jacked up the car and took the flat tire off. She got into my car with the tire and we drove back to town. After much searching we found a garage still open. Beba is a most charming person and soon had a young man who agreed to fix the tire and then drive her back to the airport. Somehow, it never occurred to us that anyone would harm us. We were both very trusting and no one did give us any trouble. The young man took her back to her car after repairing her tire. A few hours later, she was on her way back to Tuba City.

I had a head start, but a longer drive. The night was dark, the roads were icy, and so I drove with great care. My biggest problem was that I kept falling asleep, almost sliding off the road at times. At the last moment, I would awake, shake my head and go on. I sang songs, talked aloud to myself, and stopped at the occasional cafes to have a cup of coffee.

At last Crown Point and my house came in sight. I hastily carried all my loot into the house, showered and changed my clothes, then, walked up the path to the hospital to start the day with my patients. No sleep for me that night.

Finally, my nine—instead of six—months were up in Crown Point. I had applied to the Atomic Bomb Casualty Commission in Japan, where a friend of mine was working as a pediatrician. I had also applied to the BIA in Alaska. The BIA in Alaska answered first. It was easy to transfer with the government paying all of my expenses including enough for five thousand pounds worth of household goods.

It was not easy to leave all my friends in Crown Point. They gave me a wonderful farewell party, at which they presented me with a magnificent turquoise and silver necklace, which I cherish to this day.

COMING TO ALASKA

After working for nine months with the Navajo Indians in Crown Point, New Mexico, I transferred to the Territory of Alaska in March 1953. Both the work with the New Mexico Indians and the Alaska assignments were under the control of the Bureau of Indian Affairs, or BIA.

I chose to go home first to see my family in Opelika, Alabama. I drove from New Mexico to Alabama in my Plymouth automobile with my Airedale, Tinker. Whenever I stopped to eat I left Tinker in the car. On my return to the car I almost always found a crowd surrounding my car, laughing at Tinker who had moved to my seat where she sat, with her paw on the driver's wheel, looking very confident.

When I reached Opelika, where my father was a high-church Episcopal priest, I found that everyone I met thought I was absolutely crazy to go to such a rough, wild, far away, cold, and desolate country, where they'd heard the temperatures dropped way below zero and people froze to death when they stepped outside. Nonetheless, my family could not deter me from my plans because I thought that it would be a real adventure and they were kind enough after a week's visit, to drive me to Atlanta, Georgia, where I boarded a train for Seattle.

I was loaded for bear. The government allotted me five thousand pounds to move my household goods to Alaska. Since I had no household goods, I bought all the food that I figured I might need: dog food for Tinker, and many tins of coffee. I didn't drink coffee much myself but had heard that coffee was like gold in Alaska. Then I added cases of peas, beans, tomatoes, bags of rice and whatever dried food I could find.

Tinker was placed in the baggage car, and at various stops, I would get out and rescue Tinker from the baggage car to have a short walk.

It took three days to get to Seattle by train. I was lucky enough to have a sleeper on the train but felt sad that Tinker had to be kept in the baggage car. In Seattle I found a hotel that catered to the BIA personnel, left Tinker in the room, and headed for the main BIA office.

All the department heads looked askance at me. I did look much younger than my twenty-eight years. All sorts of advice was given to me, some of which consisted of information on how to run a hospital in the "Bush," which was what the area in Alaska outside of the road system was called. These people seemed to know that, though I thought I was to be stationed in the new Alaska Native Hospital in Anchorage, that the Bush would find me. They told me that if my patients ran out of meat and I wanted my patients to eat properly, I was to buy moose meat out of season from the Natives. The offenses would land me in jail if I were caught, but I was told in most definite terms that the BIA would not stand behind me if I were caught. I received tons of instructions, most of which went right over my head. Nonetheless, I took numerous packets of information from all the different department heads to read and digest later. I did try to read some of it.

Before boarding the ferry that would take me from Seattle to Juneau, the capital of Alaska, I had to go through customs, since Alaska was still a territory. I had to have a passport, believe it or not, to go to Alaska! The ferryboat on which I came north was named the Bartlett after the delegate from Alaska to the US House of Representatives. He was our only representative for the whole Alaska territory.

On board the ferry I ended up with a roommate unknown to me before the trip. She smoked nonstop. I found it was much pleasanter to stay out on deck, where the air was fresh.

Poor Tinker, my Airedale, was very lonesome. She had been assigned to the hold where all the cars were lashed down. Before we boarded the ferry, officials told me that at every stop going up the coast of Southeastern Alaska, I could take her out for a walk. However, once on board, the rules changed and there was nothing I could do to get the captain to let me rescue Tinker from the hold.

I was allowed only to go below to feed and water her, but no walks were allowed. Consequently she spent the day howling. I couldn't blame her but the other passengers kept asking, "Who owns that dog?" I kept very quiet. About nine each night, in my pajamas, I would climb down the ladder into the hold to give her some Seconal that I had with me. Gradually she would quiet down and go to sleep, only to awaken at five in the morning to begin howling again.

The trip lasted five days with frequent long stops along the coast in Ketchikan, Wrangell, Petersburg, Sitka, and finally the capital, Juneau, where we disembarked.

At the very first stop in Ketchikan, as I stepped on Alaskan soil, I felt a sense of freedom that I had never felt before. Here was a magnificent country where one could make it or not, not because of, or in spite of one's family. I knew then that I could make it. Indeed life in Alaska has been the adventure I wanted since I first got off the ferry in Ketchikan, before heading on toward Juneau, way back over fifty-five years ago.

As we waited for the freight, Tinker was unloaded in her large kennel on which my brother Stan had painted her name in large black letters, TINKER. Below this was OWNER, also in capital letters, JEAN C. PERSONS, M D. I kept very quiet and stood as far away from every one else as I could, trying not to be noticed. I was not totally successful, so was very happy to get off the ferry.

In Juneau, I was met by some of the BIA personnel who took me to the Baranof, the only good hotel in town. It was, for those days, a very fancy hotel with beautiful chandeliers in the huge reception room. This was the hotel where the legislators stayed and had their cocktail hours in the bar after their long sessions during the day.

The next day, after arranging with a nice family with a little boy to care for Tinker for a week, I met with the BIA chief for the Alaska Native Service, Dr. Ted Hynson. During this time I learned more about the workings of the Native Service and again had to sign multiple papers.

I also learned a lot from my compatriots. At my first Regional Native Service conference in Juneau, Dr. Stu Rabeau, the Medical Officer in Charge of the Kotzebue up on the western coast of Alaska, told me that all general orders from Washington DC, and Seattle, should be placed in file thirteen. He told me this when no one was in hearing distance. A big man with an imperious voice, he was called the King of Kotzebue. As time went by, I tried to follow his advice. After all, he had been in Alaska several years before me and knew the ropes.

Then I flew down to Sitka in a floatplane, my first flight on a small plane, en route to Mt. Edgecomb for a weeklong orientation. Mt. Edgecomb had a large Native boarding school as well as a four hundred-bed hospital for the more complicated medical and the orthopedic surgical problems from all over Alaska.

The town of Sitka is located on the beautiful Baranof Island southeast of Juneau. Mt. Edgecomb is on a small island out in Sitka Sound. It is in a magnificent spot. The weather, though mild most of the time, covers Sitka and Mt.Edgecomb with rain and fog many days. A ferry ran every half hour between Sitka and Mt. Edgecomb. The fare was something like 25 cents. People were constantly going back and forth.

At Mt. Edgecomb, I was met by one of the hospital emissaries, and taken first to my quarters and then to dinner. In the morning I went to the hospital where a nice young doctor showed me all around the hospital. There were many tuberculosis patients, a large number of whom had come for surgical removal of a tuberculous lung or surgery on a tuberculosis joint.

The hospital was well supplied with all sorts of specialty doctors, pediatricians, orthopedic surgeons, OB-Gyn doctors, ENT specialists, and also a dentist.

The doctors were all very nice to me, showing me around the hospital explaining how to deal with many of the medical problems they expected I would encounter.

However, it was the dentist who snagged me for my most necessary lessons. "Jean," he said, "You know all that stuff. Let me teach you about what you really need to know."

Thereupon, he went through some of the rudiments of the practice of dentistry, mostly about how to do extractions, using an instrument called an elevator, to aid me in my practice.

I hated anything to do with dentistry because as a child I had suffered greatly while undergoing treatment by dentists, who were, as I look back on them, true sadists who enjoyed inflicting pain. For years, as an adult, whenever I was placed in an upright dental chair to be treated, I would slide way down as far as I could go, in an effort to distance myself from the dentist. Nowadays, the dental assistant puts the patient in a chair that then reclines to a table, from which there is no escape.

Despite my fear of dentistry, the older, kindly dentist at Mt. Edgecomb did me a great favor in teaching me the rudiments of his profession. In the years that followed I appreciated him more and more.

Most of the time when I was not at the hospital, I lived in one of the dorm rooms set aside for single teachers and other adult staff who had no families, as well as for guests on the island. Across the hall from me lived Jim Parsons, a psychologist. With the similarity of our names, both our mail and our laundry frequently got mixed up. Some things were a bit embarrassing.

The head of the hospital, Dr. Andy Wehler, invited me over for dinner one night with his family. He had been at the village of Tanana up on the Yukon for a number of years, so had many tales to tell me about the country and the Athabaskans who lived there. He and his wife had tried for several years to get pregnant without success, but as soon as they moved to Tanana they had one baby after another. The word was, that the cause was the water of the mighty Yukon River. I was forewarned.

Prior to coming to Alaska I had been very shy, but in Sitka I got a big boost to my morale that changed my outlook on life.

Before my one week of orientation was over, one of the school-teachers asked me to marry him. Later, I found that he was planning to go to Africa and I am sure he just didn't want to go alone. My Alaska adventures had now begun.

After the orientation period was over, I flew back to Juneau to meet with the Medical Director for a few more days. I picked up Tinker from the nice family who had taken care of her, then flew on to Anchorage to be met by my Uncle Bill, who at that time was in command of the Elmendorf Air Force base. For several days I stayed with Uncle Bill and Aunt Georgia, noting that some of the privates were busy working in their house, cleaning silver and doing other tasks. They also walked Tinker for me, which made me feel rather strange. I didn't know if I should tip them or not, then decided that wouldn't be proper. Things were certainly different in the military in those days.

Uncle Bill felt a responsibility for me because my father, his older brother, had written to ask him to keep an eye on me. How he was supposed to do this with me in Tanana on the Yukon I have no idea, but he did later make a one trip to Tanana to check on me. My father also had written Bishop Gordon, the Episcopal Bishop of Alaska, in Fairbanks, to keep tabs on me. I think Poppa was a bit leery about my whole Alaskan venture.

The Alaska Native Hospital in Anchorage, known from then on as ANS Hospital, was close to completion when I arrived but not yet ready for patients. It was about three months behind schedule. Located off Third Avenue and Gambell Street, it was huge, scheduled to hold four hundred patients. It was to be the general hospital for the Natives from all over Alaska and the head nurse was to be in charge of all the nurses in the scattered Native Service hospitals in Alaska. Across from the hospital was another building, which was to house business offices, a large cafeteria and housing for the nurses and single doctors. I was scheduled to live there but when the authorities found that I had brought Tinker, they told me that I would have to live in a trailer. That was not an appealing idea. Since the hospital's completion was delayed for three months, I was given the opportunity to "man" one of the Bush hospitals, then to return to Anchorage to work in the new hospital.

It was not long before I realized that there were only a handful of doctors scheduled to be on the Anchorage hospital staff. In fact, I was the only staff doctor so far to arrive in Anchorage. I knew then that the work would be much like it was at Charity Hospital in New Orleans, when, as interns, we had to not only care for all the patients but also to do all the scut-work. I did not look forward to this idea. I chose the Bush assignment to Tanana, right in the center of Alaska.

After a few days with Uncle Bill, I was on my way to my temporary assignment. He took me to the airfield to catch a plane for Fairbanks. I think Poppa fully expected that Bishop Gordon would meet me. He didn't nor did I did think he would or should. To please my father, I did give Bishop Gordon a phone call from the airfield in Fairbanks just to tell him I had arrived. He thanked me for calling. After that, I went on into town to spend the night in the old Nordale hotel.

Eva McGowan, a charming older lady, was the official welcomer at the hotel. She had a comfortable chair and desk just inside the entrance of the hotel. She had been working there for years and could answer any question. Tinker was with me, of course, but that seemed to be no problem with the hotel manager as long as she did not bark or tear things up, so I kept her right with me even in the dining room.

My hotel room was large with two queen-sized beds. When I registered, I learned that as things got busier at night with overflow guests, someone else might be put in my room to use the other bed. The door was to remain unlocked. It was an unusual arrangement but I was in a new country and didn't feel I could object. Sharing of hotel rooms was common in those days since space was so limited. The additional guest might be of either sex. Believe me, I kept Tinker right on my bed with me. When the door opened about two or three in the morning, I held her close. She uttered a low growl, which apparently was enough for the unknown person to leave me alone. The snoring that ensued was loud and I did not sleep too well after his arrival.

The next morning I was up early, dressed in the dark, grabbed my bag and left the room quickly. To this day I have never known who or what my roommate was.

After a quick breakfast and checkout, I caught a cab out to Phillip's Field to find my plane for Tanana. Phillip's Field was a short dirt strip on the outskirts of town. There was a tiny building on the side of the dirt field with a sign on it: "Bob Byers' Flying Service." In the building was a small waiting room consisting of a desk where a lady sat going through a stack of papers, two straight-backed chairs and a small heater by the side of the desk. It gave off a lot of heat. The one window looked out on the field where a four-seat Cessna could be seen. It was the only plane on the field.

Within a few minutes after Tinker and I arrived, Bob Byers came in to give me a five minutes' warning for the flight. Bob was a pilot with whom I would fly off and on for the next few years. He never batted an eye when he saw Tinker. He first loaded my baggage into the back seat, then Tinker. Finally I got into the front seat next to Bob. Tanana was 140 miles west of Fairbanks as the crow flies.

I had worn my one good outfit, which consisted of a light blue suit, stockings and heels. I felt quite dressed up for this momentous occasion. I wanted to make a good impression on my new staff when I reached Tanana.

Bob had the mail service to Manley Hot Springs, the halfway point to Tanana, and flew this route two to three times a week unless the weather was bad or the temperature was below -25 F.

After we were well strapped in, he taxied down to the end of the runway and off into the air we flew. Never had I been in such a small plane before. It was even smaller than the Grumman Goose Amphibian that I had flown in Southeast Alaska. I found this all very exciting. Bob gave a running commentary as we flew over various landmarks and we had a brief stop in Manley Hot Springs to deliver the mail.

After over an hour of flying, he circled over a tiny village with a number of small buildings built along the banks of the great Yukon River. Here was Tanana, to be my home for the next three and a half years. I only hoped, as we landed, that I would know enough to take care of the people in this small village. The village looked very small.

We landed on the short dirt airstrip with a little Civil Aeronautics Authority (CAA) building at one end. The CAA later became the Federal Aviation Administration (FAA). Beside the building was an old black pickup truck with what seemed to be a multitude of figures standing packed in the back all waving with great vigor.

Tanana was a village of about 175 people coming and going, many in the summer going to fish camp, while in winter others were off to beaver camp. Upon landing, I got out of the plane and was trying to walk in the dignified manner befitting a new doctor. I was in heels, mind you, when Tinker hopped out of the plane behind me, running between my legs to make a dash for the truck. I tripped and almost fell. Gone was my resolve to be proper. I gave up and decided to just be myself. That's the way it was to be.

Jean and Tinker, Tanana 1953

Tanana Days

When I made the flight into Tanana with Bob Byers that first week in May 1953, I was filled with wonder as we flew over the tiny village built along the mighty Yukon River. Though it seemed so remote, 140 miles west of Fairbanks, my only hope was that I would know enough to care for all the villagers below.

An old black pickup was waiting as we landed. We met everyone, and then Tinker and I got into the front seat next to the driver, Ambrose Kosevnikoff, who was our wonderful hospital maintenance man. The rest of the group, including the head nurse, the staff nurses, the hospital aides, and the maintenance crew, were all packed standing up into the back of the pickup.

First on the dirt road going to the hospital was the CAA housing, where six CAA members lived, some of whom had families stationed with them. Next came the nurses' home, an L-shaped frame building. The nurses shared this with Jim Kimble, the chief of maintenance, his wife and kids, who lived in the smaller part of the L.

Then we came to the one-story hospital. It was whitewashed, as was the nurses' home. It had a small porch in the front, making it look like a warm and friendly place.

To the right of the hospital was my new home, a three-bedroom house with a basement containing a washer and dryer. Later, one of the Episcopal clergymen, Walter Hannum, would come to borrow my laundry facilities every week or so, since he had no such luxuries in his house. In fact, he, like most in the villagers, had neither running water nor any indoor bathroom facilities.

Behind my house was another whitewashed house where Ronnie Nusinginia the hospital electrician, lived with his family. On down the road by the river, was the schoolhouse where Arnold Griese and his family lived, and where Arnold taught forty children of all grade levels. Arnold was a fascinating man who lived in part of the school building with his wife, Jane, and his two very cute little tow-headed children, Warren and Cynthia.

From the school on down to the riverfront, was a row of log and frame cabins where most of the Athabaskan Indians lived. A Northern Commercial Company (NC) store and an Episcopal church mingled

Tanana from the air, 1953

Tanana hospital compound from the air

Jean's home, a stone's throw from the Tanana hospital

with these buildings, as did a small Catholic chapel. While Tanana had a resident Episcopal clergyman, the Catholic priest came down from Fairbanks to hold service only once a month or so.

A few whites lived in the village, some married to Natives. Ronnie Humphries lived in, and was in charge of the NC store, one of many stores in a chain of stores across Alaska. The largest NC store and base was in Anchorage. In those days, everything imaginable was sold in the store, from groceries to clothing, to various types of machinery. The NC stores bought fish, moose meat and gold from the locals, trading these for supplies.

My house was within a stone's throw of the hospital. In addition to other nice things about my house, there was indoor plumbing, a very special luxury. Visitors to Tanana often stayed with me mainly because of this addition. Not too long after I arrived, Ambrose built a fence around my house for Tinker, who loved being outside while I was at work, no matter if the temperature was down to -50 F. The Native dogs in town routinely stayed outdoors, chained on the banks of the Yukon River all year long, wearing booties only when pulling a sled or racing. These dogs were not considered as pets. They were real work dogs.

As I mentioned earlier, I had been given an allowance of 5,000 pounds for my household goods. So when I came to Tanana, I brought food: cases of beans, corn, tomatoes, peas, and most valuable of all, cases of coffee. Cases of dog food for Tinker were included. Coffee was said to be like gold in the Interior. Sure enough, when I went down to the NC store the prices were horrendous.

Despite all my supplies, I ended up eating at the hospital, which was wonderful, saving lots of time. Besides, I hated to cook.

Room and board together totaled forty dollars a month, much more economical for me. This was at a time when gas "Outside" was twenty-five cents a gallon. My salary was $1,250 dollars a month and half of this went to my brother who had dropped out of college to help support me during my medical school years. Now he could go back to school—a fair exchange.

As soon as all my baggage was in my new home, I hurried over to see the hospital. Everyone in the hospital was welcoming. The whole staff was a close-knit group, including the nursing assistants, the cooks, and the maintenance crew.

There was a small entrance to the hospital with a room to the left for the secretary, and on the right, was another small hallway with a bench on either side for the patients who came for clinic. This in turn, led into the clinic exam room and from here into the X-ray department.

On either side as we walked down the hall were two wards: on the left for the fifteen beds allocated to tuberculosis patients, and on the right, fifteen more beds in two wards, one for pediatrics and one for all the rest of the patients, pneumonias, bad fractures, infections and women in labor.

I was not ready to use the well-equipped surgery at the end of the hall. I told the nurses that if I had to do surgery, they would have to read to me out of the book. Surgery was strictly not my field. I did luck out, though, and never had to do any major operations, though we had tons of minor surgeries.

The lab was a tiny room with a table on which was a microscope. But we had no lab technician, so one of my nurses, Mary O'Tier, taught herself to do blood counts and urine exams. We had no way to do blood chemistries (glucose, cholesterol, electrolytes, and so on) or EKGs either.

Back to the main hall. This led to a large dining room where the nursing staff ate. Beyond that was a massive kitchen run by a husband and wife cooking team. In the rear of the hospital was Jim Kimble's and Ambrose Kosevnikoff's machinery area. Underneath the kitchen was a basement with a dirt floor. Here were stored meat, eggs, butter and other perishables.

In those days, we got our annual store of supplies once a year on the paddleboat, which brought everything down from the town of Nenana. The supplies came from Seattle to Seward, then moved by train to Nenana, thence down the Tanana River by paddleboat to its confluence with the Yukon River. The paddleboat was named The Nenana. The confluence was just above Tanana and from there down; the Nenana brought the supplies to the hospital.

The arrival of the boat in early July was a great occasion. Everyone in the village and all the hospital staff came out to see the paddleboat pull into the bank in front of the hospital. Planks were laid down between the boat and the bank, and the supplies were unloaded for the coming year.

The responsibility for ordering the hospital supplies lay heavily on the doctor, the head nurse, and the chief maintenance man, Jim Kimble. It was a huge job and took several weeks to determine what and how much would be needed for the following year.

By the time I arrived in May, the butter was rancid, the old eggs tasted terrible, and the meat was gone. We had Spam, baked, broiled, fried and boiled. I never want to taste Spam again. Keeping good healthy diets for the patients was difficult. However, fish were plentiful and the patients did love fish heads and fisheye soup, I did not! However, it was nourishing and helped with their protein needs.

Back in the clinic, I had a startling introduction to my exam room. On one side of the clinic table, there was a chair with a dead man sitting on it. I looked at the body, then at the head nurse, Francis Woodward, who was escorting me. She explained that he was waiting for the pilot to come to fly him home for burial. The only way he would fit in the small plane was to have him in a seated position next to the pilot so he could travel home. Perfectly reasonable, right?

My staff consisted of the head nurse, six RN's and one practical nurse. These came and went as some transferred out and others in.

One nurse I remember well was Nancy. She took care of Tinker once when I was on a field trip. Before going to my house after I returned, I saw Nancy and thanked her profusely for the good care she had given Tinker. Instead of replying she rushed away in tears. It seems that she had taken Tinker out hunting with her. When she fired her shotgun, Tinker jumped up and was hit.

With this information, I rushed home to see Tinker. She was lying on the floor bleeding copiously from a wound in her paw. I applied pressure and soon the bleeding stopped. Tinker was weak for a week, but gradually regained her strength with a lot of extra meat in her diet. Soon she was back on all fours. But Nancy was never her bouncy, cheerful self again. Though she hadn't meant to hurt Tinker, I think she did not forgive herself. She transferred out to another hospital, a great loss to us.

There had been no doctor in Tanana for nearly a year. The nurses had been taking care of the patients to the best of their ability, sending the seriously ill or injured on to St.Joseph's hospital in Fairbanks by the next available plane. Therefore, patients were used to coming to the hospital at any time during the day or night, because there was always a nurse on duty. This had to change when I arrived. I knew, as the only doctor, that I could not survive if I were called at all hours of the night, as well as working during the day. So, I set up hours for the clinic from one to four in the afternoon. The change did not sit well with anyone at first.

In the morning after breakfast, the nurses and I made rounds of the inpatients, and then we had lunch. After lunch we had clinic for three hours. In no time at all, the villagers started to come at one o'clock, setting their watches so they wouldn't be late. Remember, I was the new doctor and they didn't trust me. All the previous doctors had been men, and here I was, a woman.

On my first clinic afternoon the village men came, apparently to check me over. I must have passed inspection, because the next day the women came and on the third day, they brought the children. I was relieved when the villagers accepted me and the clinic hours.

During the summer, when it was daylight all night long, pilots would fly patients from up and down the river at any time. Most everyone had relatives in the village, so barring emergencies, they could stay with family or friends until the next afternoon clinic time. The pilots soon all knew of my schedules and relayed the information to the patients in the other villages. This helped a lot.

The first week that I was in Tanana, a man knocked on my door 2:00 a.m. I asked what his problem was. "I'm sick, that's all."

"Go over to the hospital," I told him. "The nurse will check you and if she thinks I need to see you tonight I'll come over." No nurse came to fetch me. But, I did not go to sleep from worrying about the man. In the morning I checked with the nurse.

"Oh, he had a little cold, for at least two weeks."

The patients who came to clinic in the afternoons waited on the benches in the hall by the clinic door. We saw them all in turn, barring emergencies. Patients included animals in distress: a dog with a

36

broken foot, a lynx with an injured head, and another dog after a bad dogfight with lacerations that needed to be sutured. Others had skin lesions or gastrointestinal problems. The animals waited in turn with their masters, and were seen in between the human patients. No one seemed to mind and the system worked well.

In the evenings after dinner, we all would play with the children. Everyone had a favorite, but no child was left out. In the summer we would take all the children who were well enough across the road in front of the hospital to the grassy area beside the rushing Yukon River. There we would all play together. It was a happy time.

Of course, we took emergencies at any time, night or day, delivering babies whenever they decided to arrive.

One morning a lovely lady from Kaltag was sitting on the clinic bench knitting a baby blanket when I went over to the hospital. She looked perfectly comfortable.

"Hi, good morning, are you okay? What are you doing, are you having any pains, any bleeding?" I asked.

"No doctor, no pains, no problems," she said. "You told me to come have my baby during the daytime, so I came this morning." Needless to say, she had her baby that night. Statistics show that most babies are delivered during the day, but I've never believed them, certainly not in my practice!

The obstetric patients were extraordinary, especially compared with my white patients. The only way they showed signs of pain was with drops of perspiration on the nose. Not one ever yelled or complained in any way. I've always had the greatest admiration for them, even before I had my own three kids. The kids were wonderful too. Often I gave the shots when the nurse was busy. Not one ever cried. A little tear might trickle down a cheek, then, "Thank you, doctor." I felt so bad because I knew the shot had hurt. The Native kids were amazing, not like the white kids who howled.

Sometimes we ran out of beds. Then Ambrose would find wooden crates for the tiny babies. We even used cardboard boxes when we ran out of the crates. At other times, we put two children with the same diagnosis in the same crib.

The children came in with pneumonia, severe anemias, and injuries of all sorts. They responded to the medical treatments as well as to all the loving care that all the staff gave them. After sending some of the children back to their villages after they were well, I soon learned to keep them for longer periods just to build up their general health. This way, the kids were not back again in the hospital shortly after discharge with another illness.

Not too long after working in the hospital, being happy to send them home with more weight, I found that some of the parents were not happy because the children were pale after being in the hospital, out of the sun for so long. However, as soon as they were home for a bit they regained their color when they were again outside much of the time.

Within a few weeks of my arrival, one of the pilots brought in a little one-year-old girl from Ruby who had been trapped by a dog team that was chained down by the river. She was scalped, literally, and the dogs had chewed on her for at least five minutes before anyone was able to separate the dogs to save her. The lead dog had grabbed her and pulled her in so all the dogs could reach her. Some of the Natives and then her parents heard her screaming and were finally able to get her away from the dogs.

Luckily, a pilot was in the village. Quickly they wrapped her up and within a half hour they were in Tanana. The head nurse and I took her into the clinic exam room, cleaned her wounds, staunched the bleeding, checking her with care. In my training at Charity Hospital in New Orleans, I had always been taught never to suture a dog bite, but here was this beautiful child with her scalp split open, laid all the way to the back of her head, the neck muscles on the left torn were severed. Every time she exhaled, the air would bubble through the tear in her neck, meaning that her trachea had been lacerated. She had a few bites on her face but these were minor. On her back, she had multiple bites.

I started to suture her, putting her back together as best I could. She was in such terrible shape I knew she would never survive, but the nurse and I kept working on her. It took three hours before everything was in place. All during this time the parents sat on the little bench outside of the exam room with the pilot. Finally we were through and she was still alive. With an IV going and her head, neck, and back all bandaged up, we carried her out, first for her parents to see, then down to the children's ward. We watched her all night. In the morning, she awakened, smiled just a bit. From then on, with her parents coming up from her village to see her frequently, she recovered rapidly and in six days went home. Amazingly, the scars on her face and back disappeared. Her hair covered the scalp scars. Only the neck scars were minimally visible and she later grew into a beautiful young woman.

The pilot went downriver after he took the parents home that first day. As he went, he stopped at the other villages, and told them, "The new doc is okay." If things had not gone well, and by logic, they should not have, I probably would not have had any of the villagers come to the hospital.

As new nurses came to Tanana I would try to train them for the times when I was out on a field trip or on an emergency trip to one of the villages. One nurse was Daisy Glidden, who had been at St.Mary's boarding school with me in New York, years before. This was the school where I had been sent for high school when my mother was dying. Daisy had signed up with the ANS and requested to be assigned to Tanana to work with me.

Trying to teach Daisy how to deliver a baby was not easy. Just before I left on an emergency trip, I checked in to see how she was doing with a patient in good labor. There Daisy stood, at the end of the delivery table, in a stance that was exactly like a football player waiting to receive the ball. Quickly I called the head nurse to take over. I will never forget the picture Daisy made.

One of the best things that happened shortly after I came to Tanana was a visit from a pilot by the name of Garfield Hansen. We always called him just "Hansen." He had been teaching flying in Fairbanks, but was getting bored doing this. He came to me with a proposal. If I would use him for the Tanana hospital trips, he would charge me $25 an hour for the use of his Piper Family Cruiser, at a time when the going rate was $35 an hour. The plane had four seats and had big wheels for landing on short fields. Without any further discussion, I accepted.

Hansen flew back to Fairbanks and put his trailer on a barge to float it down to Tanana. Arnold Griese, the school teacher, let him put his trailer right next to the schoolhouse. Then Arnold hooked him up with the school's water supply, the heating system and the electricity. Neither Arnold nor I consulted our superiors. We knew what we needed and we did not have to go through all the rigmarole that we would have had to go through nowadays. Everyone in the village was happy to have pilot Hansen in Tanana.

Soon after I took over the hospital, I learned that there would be a radio call to the villages every afternoon at three. Since I had never talked on a radio before, the idea scared me. At first, I had no problem. I had a list of the villages and a list of the medications that the government supplied each village. The medications were posted on the wall by the radio.

Radio call was essential in Alaska, since we had no telephones, or cell phones, and no village was connected to another by road. Communication between villages, other than radio, was by boat in the summer, by dog team in the winter, or airplane, if one was available. Radio was the lifeline for the whole territory of Alaska.

I would start my calls each afternoon with, "KWG53, Tanana calling KWG51, Minto, KWG53 Tanana, calling KWG51 Minto," repeatedly. With no reply, I would go on to call the rest of the village call numbers.

The teacher, local clergyman, or the grocer took the calls in each village. Since there had not been a doctor at the hospital for a good while, no one in the villages was taking the medical call. However, when they realized there was a doctor in Tanana, calls started to be answered. When that first booming voice answered me, I was petrified. I took a deep breath and answered in a quivery voice.

The voice said, "A little boy has a fever of 105 degrees and a very sore throat.

"Oh", I said, "he needs to be seen." Then I found that the village was about sixty miles away. The weather was bad and no plane would fly. After a few more questions, I ordered medications from the list on the wall, and then made some common-sense recommendations. The next day when I called, it was a great relief to know the child was much improved.

Gradually I became more comfortable with the radio. When I went to Juneau for a medical conference, I asked the director of the BIA, Dr. Ted Hynson, what area I was to cover. He said, "Any village that contacts you on the radio for medical help is yours." Did that ever make a difference in my planning and my life!

I came to find out that I was responsible for the healthcare in eighteen other scattered villages besides Tanana, none of which were connected by road. They varied in size from twelve people up to two hundred and fifty people in size and covered an area larger than the state of Colorado. They were located on the Yukon, the Tanana, and the Koyukuk Rivers. My territory included all the villages below Fort Yukon down to and including Kaltag on the lower Yukon River, a distance of 300 miles. Also included were all of the villages on the Koyukuk River and a few more up the Tanana River. Further north, we extended up to Wiseman and to my northernmost village, Anaktuvak Pass, the latter an Eskimo village being one of the most nomadic in Alaska. It was located in the Brooks Range halfway between Fairbanks and Barrow. This village was unique in that the Eskimos there had no marine food sources. They subsisted mainly on caribou as the herds made their way south, and fish from the nearby freshwater lake, with a few greens in the summer.

About the same time, the Juneau ANS office sent me my job description. It stated that I should make rounds every morning with the head of the hospital, sharing night and weekend call with my fellow physicians, and confer with them about the care and treatment of the patients.

I wrote back that every morning I conferred with me, myself, and I, that I was the MOC and the only doctor. The next mail brought me a letter from Juneau that gave me an increase in salary, from $1,250 dollars a month to $1,500 dollars.

I found life in Tanana very exciting. One adventure was literally hot. In August 1953, we had a tremendous fire. Five thousand acres burned. It all started after a very dry spring. An electrical storm set off a few sparks and these grew into a tremendous blaze. By evening, three fires were going and the smoke was so thick we could barely see or breathe. Of course, we had no fire department in Tanana. None of my villages did. Therefore, the CAA called the Forestry Departments in Fairbanks and Anchorage.

Our hospital maintenance crew had already started bulldozing back of the hospital when the Anchorage Fire Department flew in

20,000 feet of hose and pumps. With this amount of hose, we could utilize the Yukon River if we needed to and we did. Firemen came in to Tanana from both Anchorage and Fairbanks and organized the bulldozing. At the hospital, we were busy making sandwiches and coffee, and all night we carried these out to the fire fighters. The permafrost was just one foot below the surface, but the fire spread under the tundra rapidly.

The CAA again contacted Fairbanks at my request, and I ordered plasma and other medical supplies that we did not have on hand, in case of any bad burns. I treated minor burns and injuries on the spot.

For three more days, the area got hotter and hotter. A Globe-master from Fairbanks flew in on the third day of the fire, bringing an Army cat-skinner and another huge Cat. The cooks knocked themselves out getting food out for the men.

On our breaks, from looking out for the fire fighters needs, we listened to reports on the radio, learning that our village, the hospital, and the CAA installations were about to be wiped out. A C-54 at Ladd Field was standing by, ready to evacuate the hospital, CAA personnel, and all the villagers. It was an exciting time. When we did sleep, we all slept in our clothes, ready to move at a moment's notice. The firemen all slept in shifts, in the tents that they had brought with them.

On the fourth night, the flames were only a hundred yards back of the hospital, leaping up some 400 feet in the sky. We were busy preparing the patients, getting ready for evacuation, when suddenly the wind shifted and it began to rain. The fire died slowly, but the firemen stayed for another four days to be sure the fire was completely out, because the tundra smolders and the fire could easily flare up again suddenly, unless completely put out.

Everyone was exhausted, but happy, though hair, clothes, and everything, were full of smoke. It took weeks for things to get back to normal and get the smell of smoke out of our systems and out of our clothes. Our only real casualty was our pilot, Hansen, who got a bad burn on his right hand, but with prompt treatment he healed quickly.

With Hansen based in Tanana, we could make dependable field trips, which were always rewarding. We had eighteen villages, from those on the Tanana River, to those on the Koyukuk River, to those on the Yukon River including Beaver on down to and including Kaltag. Of course, there were two villages not on a river, Wiseman and Anaktuvak Pass, the latter of which was one of my favorites.

On some weekends, Bishop Gordon would fly down from Fairbanks to take me up to Fort Yukon to hold clinic. Here was a beautiful old hospital, the Hudson Stuck Memorial Hospital named after an Episcopal priest who, in the very early days, had climbed Mt. Denali, otherwise known as Mt. Mckinley. He was involved in other explorations of Alaska as well.

There were no doctors at the Hudson Stuck Hospital so Bishop Gordon was happy to have a volunteer doctor come see some of the people in the clinic there. Later Dr. Don Palmer from Alabama, came up with his family to work and care for this village.

My whole area was huge but the population overall was very small and periodically I was notified by Juneau that an uncovered area needed a doctor. Therefore, I had extra trips to Tok, and to Eagle, to hold clinic for the people there.

Eagle was a village with two sections, one with mostly whites and the other nearby part where the Natives lived, along with some white-Native mixed families. After our clinics were over in Eagle, Hansen, the nurse, and I decided to make a trip to Dawson, where Robert Service had lived. It was very close to Eagle, but across the border in Canada. We had a lot of fun wandering around the deserted town with its old saloons and dance halls. There were pictures on the walls outside the buildings of the dance-hall girls in what then were very risqué costumes. We slept in a big old frame hotel with large rooms, no locks on the doors. The nurse and I slept in one room and Hansen had his room right across the hall.

In the morning, we went out to the airfield, but found that we had to have identification to cross the border back into Alaska. The nurse had hers, but I never carried a purse or even a wallet as I traveled around on my clinics. Hansen had to do some fast-talking to get the custom officers to let me go back to Alaska. It was a fun trip.

Village life had several interesting characteristics. One that still exists in many places is the lack of running water. In fact, even in this modern day, thirty percent of the villages still have no running water, so they still have to use honey buckets. For water, the Natives had to go down to the river. They carried the water up in buckets. In the winter, they first had to cut a hole in the ice that could be ten or more inches in depth. Then they lowered the bucket to get the water. Often they brought dog teams down to the river using the sled to carry the water, thus making the trip back to the cabin a little bit easier.

Everyone was supposed to boil the water before drinking it because there were so many contaminants in the water. Many of the babies who drank untreated water got severe diarrhea, and some died of dehydration without medical help.

In the hospital, I had a tough time getting fluids into the babies to replace their fluid loss at first. I had had no training up to that point in my career in threading tiny needles into the babies' tiny veins. So, I put a larger needle into the bone and gave the infusion through the bone marrow. I always would sit by the side of the babies all during the infusion time because the infusions often would clot and I would have to clear the clot right away so the fluids would continue to flow. This often took hours, but worked well.

When Hansen flew me into the villages, many of the community members met the plane, walking down the narrow path from the village. Someone almost always brought a wheelbarrow that we could use to load our supplies. This was essential when we took our heavy X-ray machine.

One of my nurses, Mary O'Tier, was a whiz at taking X-rays. She would take chest-Xrays in one room wearing her lead apron, while I would check and treat the villagers in another. As a result of these visits we were able to locate many of the active tuberculosis patients.

At first we just kept lists of the tuberculosis patients so we could notify the patient when a bed in Mt. Edgecomb or in Tanana or in an Outside sanatorium came open. Some of the patients came to Tanana for other problems, but when the chest X-ray showed one or more big tuberculosis cavities we would try to find a hospital bed for the patient. If there was one available, we would send the patient off immediately. We did not have funds to send the patient back to the village first to say good-bye to the family. Looking back, I realize this was often inhumane, because the patients would be gone sometimes for years. The only positive thing I can say is that getting the patient into the hospital saved many lives.

44

Soon we had plans to make an official field trip to each of the villages at least every six weeks. The first year we took X-rays of all the Natives who came to be checked, thus finding what a tremendous amount of tuberculosis existed in our villages.

In addition, the amount of dental work was horrendous, but by counting the number of teeth that I pulled on each trip, and sending the report to my boss in Juneau, we managed to get a dentist in Tanana after my first year.

The first dentist did not stay long. We had all been so excited at the idea of having a dentist and had set aside a room for him with all the necessary equipment. I reveled in the idea that most of my time in the villages could now be spent on medical care, rather than on the extractions that I had to do with all the toothaches. A toothache was usually the first complaint when I saw a patient. I had to take care of this problem before I could do any of the medical work.

Teeth had been good before the white man came to Alaska bringing in soda pops and candy. Now the teeth were in a sorry state. It was a rare village that had had a dentist visit. Even today, in 2007, there is a major problem when someone in the village has a toothache. If there were someone trained in the village to do extractions and other more minor work as is done in Australia with especially trained technicians, many of the Natives would not have to suffer, waiting for a dentist to come to the village or waiting to save up enough money to fly into the closest city.

Our long awaited new dentist came over to my house after he settled in and had dinner at the hospital on his first day in Tanana. He sat down in my easy chair and smiled.

"Jean," he said, "I don't drink."

"Odd statement," I thought. "Why is he telling me this?"

Of course, he turned out to be an alcoholic, running away from his past. He lasted a week before he decided to leave. His decision saved me from the unpleasant duty of firing him. It was another long wait before another dentist was recruited for Tanana.

Tuberculosis was a problem that continues into present day, not only in the Bush, but also in all the small villages all over Alaska as well as in the cities. Back then, the X-rays we took on our field trips went down to Anchorage so that Dr. Karola Reitlinger, the petite German radiologist, could read them. Of course, I had a chance to review them in Tanana prior to sending them south, thus seeing many with cavities in the lungs.

I have to share one story about Dr. Reitlinger. When I came into Anchorage once with my Michele as a baby, Dr. Reitlinger invited me for dinner. When we arrived, Michele was sleeping soundly, so she told me to just put her on her bed. I went into the bedroom and fixed Michele on the bed with pillows so she wouldn't roll off. Then I looked up on the wall above the bed. There was the head and skin of her dog. Dr. Reitlinger came in, saw my surprise and said, "That was my little dog. When she died I couldn't bear to be parted from her, so I had the taxidermist fix this so she could always be with me." I can't remember what I said. In fact I didn't know what to say except that I, too, loved my dog.

One woman who lived in a village just a little way down the Yukon had twelve children. Every one of them had some variety of tuberculosis, mostly in the lung, but some with meningitis or in the joints, all of tubercular origin. On her exam when she came to be examined, we found she had a large draining node on her neck. We took cultures, sending these down to the Anchorage ANS Hospital lab for evaluation. It took six weeks for us to get the results. These showed that her neck lesion was full of tuberculosis bacteria. We finally had the reason why all of her children had tuberculosis. She had nursed each child and with no knowledge of her disease, had infected each child.

Another source of infection in various homes was from the grandmother, who held and rocked each new baby, while the mother did the cooking and general house care. When we checked the grandmother, who had a frequent cough, we would find that she had pulmonary tuberculosis. She had passed her tuberculosis bacteria on to each new baby.

It was a long time before we had enough beds in the state to take in all the active tuberculosis patients, but after the Anchorage ANS Hospital opened up, we were finally able to get most of the patients needing hospitalization into care.

Then the government back in Washington decided to start working with Isoniazid (INH) experimentally. Half the village would get

46

INH, an anti-tuberculosis drug, while the other half of the villagers got a placebo (a pill with no medication in it). They took one of my staff nurses, Birgit Dahlstrom, to run the program in my Tanana area. Since she no longer was a staff nurse in Tanana, she wasn't eligible for a room in the Nurses' home. So, she moved into mine because I had three bedrooms, where there was plenty of room. This worked out well because she traveled a lot to the villages, and I was often on a field trip or an emergency flight when she was home. It was also nice to have someone in the house with Tinker when I was away.

Later the government carried out similar studies when I was out in Bethel. Soon it was apparent that by giving INH as a preventive medication, the tuberculosis infection rate was cut way down.

In each village on our field trips, after the nurse and I got set up to work, we would have all the little boys come in for their check ups. Then they would act as runners for us. They would get the mothers and babies, then the rest of the school children, then the men. After we saw all these patients, pulled teeth, and did general medical checks and treatments, we would go to the cabins to see the old people and others who could not get make it to the school or wherever we were holding clinic. We would stay and work until every one in the village who wanted to be checked had been seen.

Often when I went to a village, the Arctic Research doctors in Anchorage would ask me to collect specimens for their investigative work. So, we would bring back blood samples, stool, and urine samples. Trying to keep things from freezing when the weather was so very cold was not easy. Often Hansen would put the samples in his jacket pocket to keep them warm until we got back to Tanana.

If only I had been rich I could have had a very large family. As I went to the different villages time after time on regular scheduled visits or emergencies, and as the people got to know me, many of them offered me a child or two, particularly when they had eight or nine already. One of my favorites was little Percy Wholecheese. He had been in and out of the hospital a number of times, always going home healthy and happy. As I recall, he came from Koyukuk, the village below Huslia. As we were leaving one time, his mother came out to the plane with little Percy in her extended arms and said, "You take him doctor. You take such good care of him." It was tremendous and a tough decision, but I thanked her and told her I knew that he would be much happier staying with her.

Arnold Griese was one of my favorite people in the village. It was difficult to see how he could teach and handle forty kids of various ages and grades all at once in that one large schoolroom. He would give me sage advice when I needed it. He was the one who had helped Hansen get safely hooked up in his trailer with heat, water, and all the necessities so that he could live right next to the school house, close to the hospital, and thus be available when we needed him at the hospital for our many trips out in the Bush.

One time Arnold and Hansen decided to go sheep hunting. I don't remember where they went, but they did get their sheep up on a mountain. They skinned it and cut it into the appropriate pieces, then started to pack the sheep out on their backs. Arnold began to feel weak, so Hansen ended up packing most of the sheep down on his back, as well as supporting Arnold as they stumbled down the mountain..Both Arnold and Hansen were on the lean side. After getting the sheep and all their hunting equipment back in the plane, they flew back to Tanana where Arnold was about done in. They called me and quickly I went down to the schoolhouse where I found Arnold in shock, with a tender abdomen and bleeding below. After I started an IV, Hansen flew him into Fairbanks to St. Joseph's Hospital. There he was able to get several blood transfusions, which revived him in a short time. Then he had to be on a special diet. At that time we had none of the today's great ulcer medications and also we didn't know that a bacteria had caused his ruptured peptic ulcer.

Fortunately Arnold was a hardy soul and soon returned to work, but the BIA sent him a teacher by the name of Katherine who gave him some relief. He had done yeoman's work with all those kids all by himself up to that point.

Downriver, Toughy Edgington and his wife had a gold mine. He had crashed in January of '54 with his wife and a 54-year-old Native woman and all three had recovered well from this accident. I describe this event in a separate chapter later in this book. About a year later we got a distress call from him by radio to the CAA saying that his wife, who was five month's pregnant, had begun to bleed. Hansen and I flew down as soon as we could gather all the supplies needed for a very premature delivery. Normally Toughy would have flown his wife up himself, but his crashed plane was still undergoing repair, so he had no transportation.

When we got to his mine I checked his wife. She was not bleeding badly, so we put her into Hansen's plane and flew straight to Fairbanks and good old St. Joseph's hospital. Non-natives were not eligible for care in the ANS Hospitals except for emergencies. Besides this, the care for such a preemie in Tanana would not have been anything near what St. Joseph's could offer: equipment and an OB specialist for her. We got her to Fairbanks in good shape and she did not lose her baby. Later they gave me a huge gold nugget. Toughie and his wife were happy to have their baby delivered months later in Fairbanks at full term because of this emergency trip.

* * * * * * * * * *

An important part of my work at Tanana, at least to my way of thinking, was to keep the nurses happy. If happy, they would stay. If not, they would not. Without them the hospital could not run.

Therefore, whenever I was on a clinic trip to one of the villages or on an emergency flight, or if I were in Fairbanks for some reason or other, I would take note of any eligible-appearing young men. If they seemed to be nice, I would issue an invitation to come to Tanana on the next Saturday night for a dance.

If it were summertime, I would invite them to come early for a picnic. Of course, in the summer when it was light all night, it really didn't matter what time they came because we could have a picnic at any time, following it up with a dance in the nurses' home or sometimes up at the CAA in their large meeting room. In the summertime, we had to pull down all the shades to give some semblance of darkness, but coming out of a dance at three or four in the morning was a bit tough. The bright sunlight was not complimentary to one's appearance.

The dances were fun and were chaperoned by the head nurse, in theory, though one of the head nurses probably needed more chaperoning than did anyone else. Therefore, I took over. Most everyone behaved properly, so it was rare that there had to be any disciplining done. Occasionally a young man would not be invited back.

About four in the morning of every dance I would sit down on the sofa with my shears and, one by one, each of our guests would come over, sit on the floor while he received a hair cut. Since I knew only one cut, each young man sported a crew cut when he left. I thought them most becoming.

About six in the morning, we would climb into the old black hospital pickup and drive down to the airfield, where our sleepy friends climbed aboard whatever aircraft they had arrived in, and fly away.

In the summer, we often went hunting for ptarmigan, in the fall for moose. We never got anything when I was in the hunting group because I do not like to kill things. I made sure to make plenty of noise, so the animals or birds would have warning of our approach. Consequently, when anyone was serious about hunting they didn't invite me. I went along just for the fun of being outdoors.

On Saturday afternoons up at the CAA, we had three-reel movies mailed in from Fairbanks. Everyone who was free would go from the hospital to join the CAA families. One time, running back from the CAA to my house on a -50º F night taught me a lesson. All down my throat, into my trachea and even into my lungs, I could feel the crackling of ice particles. I did not do that again. This time I was a quick learner.

We often went blueberry picking when the berries were ripe in the fall. Evidence of bears abounded: large paw prints, scat, and trampled brush. They never bothered us and it never occurred to any of us that they would, so we never carried a gun. When the Coast and Geodetic Survey groups came to Tanana to do their work, they would never move out of their camp without at least one good-sized gun, a .30-O6 rifle.

In the summer, there was always someone to take us out in one of the motorboats to fish. We were supposed to have a fishing license, but I do not recall anyone who had one. It was amazing that not one of us was ever caught. There were many stories of the Fish and Wildlife men coming out of nowhere in a floatplane, landing, catching, and fining anyone fishing without a license.

The big deterrent to fishing was the presence of a multitude of mosquitoes: huge, buzzing and clouding the sky with their numbers. They came in swarms that no amount of vitamin C or B1, or any stuff rubbed on the skin or clothes could help. In fact, the mosquitoes seemed to thrive on any such additives. The only way to get away from them was to hop back into the boat and zip away down the river.

Picnics on the bluff a mile down the Yukon River from the hospital were lots of fun. We had one almost every weekend in the summer, making sure any VIP's from Washington who came to check on the hospital and us were invited.

For our picnics, we would make a big fire, roast our hot dogs and hamburgers, marshmallows and add whatever other food we could scrounge from the hospital or find at the Northern Commercial Company. We always had soft drinks and beer. We sang songs, told stories, and at the end of the picnic, the last thing we did was wash each other's hair with beer. What a mess that was, but it was tradition. Even the VIPs didn't seem to mind.

A very special dance early one fall evening in 1955 ended in tragedy. We bid good-bye to five of the boys flying in a helicopter back to their base. We had such a great time with them, but we who were due to return to work at the hospital at 6 a.m. knew it was time to say farewell. Everybody climbed into the old pickup to go down to the airstrip where we said good-bye.

It was just three hours later that the CAA sent one of their men down the road to the hospital to talk to me. Apparently, the boys had decided to stop in one of the villages on their way home to continue partying. When they got back into their helicopter, something went terribly wrong with their take-off. No sooner was the helicopter in the air, then it crashed, and all five of the boys were decapitated. All of us were in total shock and it took a long time to get over this. I still cringe when I think of that night and can just imagine the shock to their families when they received the news.

Bob Byers' mail delivery was a big event once or twice a week depending on the weather. Everyone was excited over the possibility of a letter or a package from Outside. We shared the contents of the letters as well as the packages with one another. At Christmas, we had a tree in the hospital, one in the nurses' home and a third one in my house. With the temperature running between -40°F to -60°F, the trees were sometimes rather brittle. With each stroke of the axe needles would fall from our spindly spruce trees and by the time our trees were cut,

51

there would be few needles left. We took them back, decorated them with home made ornaments, hung a bit of tinsel on the branches and thought our trees were beautiful.

Christmas music came from scratchy records on the wind-up Victrola. Rarely we could get an audible radio station from Fairbanks on our AM radio. At Christmas time there was no holiday music, but at Easter time we usually were able to get Christmas music. Easter music generally came in the early summer. I had the only radio in the hospital complex so everyone came over to my house to listen to whatever we could get. The radio station in Fairbanks got canned music and other programs sent up from Washington State. These were always several months late.

For clothes, we used to order from the Sears Roebuck catalogue. Often things did not fit and since most of us hated to rewrap the clothes to return to Sears for exchange, we would have a party, each of the nurses and I would try on each other's purchases and someone was bound to find a good fit.

We all worked hard and played hard. We made our own fun.

Just after I had finally settled myself in Tanana, my boss in Juneau sent a message that I could head south to work in Anchorage now that the hospital building was completed. It did not take more than a moment for me to decide that there was no way I was going back to the largest city in Alaska. In Tanana I was the Medical Officer in Charge (MOC) and only doctor. I loved the Athabaskans with whom I worked, and I had my own house with a yard for Tinker. It was no problem for me to say, "Thanks, but no thanks." I preferred to stay in Tanana. There I had some of the happiest and most adventuresome days of my life.

Tanana Hospital Children

Playful Airedale Tinker in Jean's yard

Newborn Stanford Gurtler in his mother's arms leaving the Tanana hospital. One of a number of babies that Jean named after her brother.

Yearly hospital supplies for the Tanana hospital coming in on the Nenana paddlewheel boat

Our new fancy hospital ambulance coming off the barge from Nenana

Truck towing Arnold Griese's airplane, which had been stuck in the muddy Tanana airfield

Jean and head nurse Dorothy Bennett with military visitors, 1955

Tuberculosis patient wearing mask as he gets ready to fly to Fairbanks, then to Anchorage for long-term hospitalization

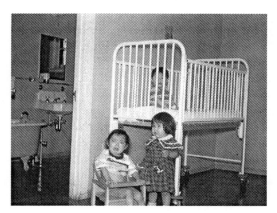

Little pediatric kids on the ward in the Tanana hospital

*Jean and Tinker getting ready to go for a ride in
Cy Hetherington's Stinson airplane*

Ambrose Kozevnikoff, great Tanana hospital maintenance man

Brother Stan and Bishop Gordon in front of St. James church

Norman Elliott gassing up his Piper Pacer to take small patient in Jean's arms back to her village of Huslia

Poppa with Coleman Inge and Randy Mendleson in front of Norman Elliott's Piper Pacer, 1955

ENT team from University of Washington arriving in Tanana for the tonsillectomy clinic

Nurse and Jean on the way to church

Jean on the front porch of Tanana ANS hospital

Tanana hospital children

Jean found some little puppies in the woods

*Taking a little patient with a head injury from Hughes to Tanana
for further care*

Jean and Tinker

Northern Commercial store in Tanana burning to the ground, 1955

Tanana staff dining room. Jean helping
Jim Kimble, chief maintenance man, with his coffee.

Nurses' mukluks all lined up

St. James church, Tanana

Timmy James with Tinker, visiting me in 1955

Cy Hetherington lifting his Stinson plane before the crash, 1953

Mary O'Tier, Mercia Kallock, pilot Cy Hetherington, and "pillowcase" meds getting ready to fly to Fairbanks, 1954

Jean with little patients in Tanana

Hansen gassing up his float plane

Hansen with Toddy Kozevnikoff, the son of Ambrose, with their bear skin

Arnold Griese, schoolteacher, with his dog

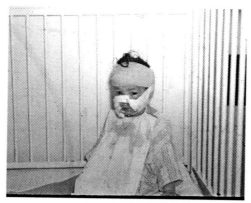

Baby from Ruby, all bandaged up after being put back together
after her severe mauling by the dog team

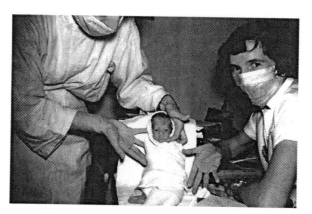

Nurse, Jean, and brand new premature

Our little hospital patients getting some sun

Daisy Glidden and head nurse Dorothy Bennett on steps to Jean's house

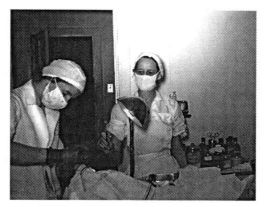

Head nurse, Francis Woodward, and Jean at work in the clinic

Jean meeting Andy Anderson's plane bringing in children from Anaktuvuk Pass for the tonsillectomy clinic

65

Ronnie Nusinginya with Jean and a fresh salmon caught in the hospital fishwheel

Basco Minook laying out the salmon caught in the hospital fishwheel

Brother Stan and the Kimble family walking home from church, 1956

Some of our young hospital patients

Getting the dogs ready for the Tanana dog races

Tanana dog races on the frozen Yukon River

Hospital crew and Long John Anderson from the CAA having a picnic at "The Point," a mile south of the hospital on the banks of the Yukon River, where we had had our weekly picnics in the summer.

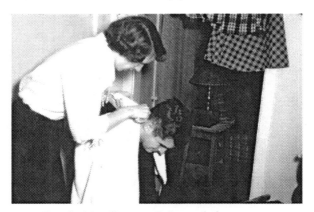

Randy Mendlesson, Episcopal clergyman, getting his monthly haircut from Jean

Carol Brandes and Jean going out on a fishing trip, 1953

The dance hall in Dawson, Canada,
on a side trip from our field trip to Eagle, Alaska, 1955

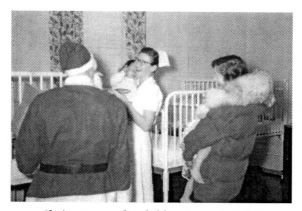

Christmas on the children's ward, 1953

Christmas in my house with Usto Schulz and Dorothy Bennett, 1955

Jean in front of Hudson Stuck Memorial Hospital in Ft. Yukon, 1954

Episcopal church in Ft. Yukon, 1954

HUSLIA

Early in the spring of 1953, shortly after I had come to Alaska, I was on a trip to Bettles. Before leaving Bettles in the afternoon about 3:30 p.m., we received a call from Hughes relaying a message from Huslia that there was a very sick man in the village. The village of Huslia, with a population of less than a hundred, was about 100 miles further down the Koyukuk River from Hughes and 150 miles northwest of Tanana. Andy Anderson was my pilot on this trip. As usual, we packed my medical supplies into the plane in their pillowcase containers.

We landed in the small village of Huslia about 5 p.m. A good many of the Natives came out to meet us. The villages had no movie house or other source of entertainment, so any time a plane came in, almost everyone who was free would hurry down the trail to the airstrip to see who was coming in. Most knew the sound of Andy's plane. He was popular with all the people up and down the rivers and in the Interior, so there were many smiling faces to greet us.

It was my first visit to Huslia. The villagers were curious once they knew that the new doctor from Tanana was on board. Almost always someone brought a wheelbarrow along in case there were supplies to be taken into the village, so I gratefully put my pillowcases into the wheelbarrow.

First, we went to the one-room schoolhouse where we met the teacher. He was a young single man who seemed delighted to have company and agreed to have us put our things in the school. Then we all made the short walk to the store. The owner was an older Caucasian man who had married one of the Native women, a warm-hearted lady who was obviously glad that someone had come to check her husband. He was sitting in an easy chair, noticeably ill, coughing copiously and running a high fever. After getting sufficient history and a brief exam, it was easy to diagnose pneumonia. Out from my bag came a needle and syringe along with a bottle of penicillin. I gave him a whopping injection along with a bottle of cough medicine. Instructions were given to his wife to be sure he received plenty of fluids: tea, soups, water. He was too ill and the weather was not good enough to fly him into Fairbanks. As a non-Native, he was not eligible for care in the

Native Hospital in Tanana except under a major emergency, even if the weather had been good.

It was getting dark by the time our visit was over, so we decided to stay in Huslia for the night in case he got worse. His wife was to call me if there was any change.

The village, like all the villages under my care, had no restaurant or hotel, just the Native log and frame homes and the store, which served as a post office as well. The only place to stay was with the teacher. He was happy to offer us an invitation.

His sleeping quarters consisted of a tiny room with a curtain hanging between the schoolroom and his room. It contained a dresser, small closet, and a narrow single bed. This room was separated from the small kitchen on the right by another hanging curtain. The three of us were to share the space. After much discussion, the teacher took the mattress into the schoolroom and placed it by the small stove that kept the schoolroom warm. He had to feed it all during the night with wood from the pile just inside the door to the outside. Andy went back to the plane for his sleeping bag that he put on the other side of the stove. I got the bedroom with what was left of the bed, the springs. The teacher took one blanket, I got the other. I must say, it was a long night with the springs hitting me first here, then there, so I moved as little as I could.

Before going to bed and after a reasonable dinner that the teacher made for us, I took a trip to the outdoor facilities taking along a flashlight. Early on, after my arrival in Tanana, I had heard of fur seats for the outhouses. Never had I given much thought to this bit of equipment, which I just thought was a bit of folklore, but when I flashed my light on the one-holer at least two inches of solid ice was on the seat. My understanding increased immediately. Lots of hemorrhoids could be accounted for.

In the morning I was up early. I went into the kitchen, poured some water from a pail into a bowl. First I washed my face, then had a bit of a body wash. The water was icy, so fortunately my ablutions were brief. I was busy brushing my teeth when I suddenly realized that I was not alone. I looked behind me and there coming through the back door, along with a cold draft, was a file of students who were very curious to see what was going on. Before the door was shut, there were forty kids of all ages supervising my every move. Fortunately by then I had on my jeans and shirt.

After a most appreciated breakfast made by the teacher, I went over to the store to see my patient. He was definitely much better, coughing less and his fever was down. Another shot of penicillin was given, a number of penicillin tablets were left for him to take. He was no longer in danger, so I did not feel bad about leaving him and going back to Tanana. He had a very cute son of about nine who was very helpful. Many years later, this small boy, by the name of John Sackett, would be very active in politics in Juneau.

As I walked back to the schoolhouse, the ice fog that had been very light earlier in the morning had become extremely dense. By the time I reached the schoolhouse, the tiny icy pellets were stinging my cheeks, and when Andy walked out of the door he said that there was no way that he could fly. School was out because it was Saturday, so all of us, Andy, the school kids, the teacher, and I played volleyball. It was great fun. We played for several hours. After lunch I held a small clinic for anyone who wanted to be seen, then we all played volleyball some more. Everyone was relaxed. There was no way to get out, so we enjoyed forced rest. The next morning my patient was continuing to improve, but he got one more shot of penicillin just to be on the safe side.

The weather did not improve. We had another day of visiting around the village, talking to everyone who was free and playing more volleyball. I was sure we would all have faces covered with red spots from all the ice fog hitting us in the face, but nothing showed. On the third day the fog lifted and Andy was able to take off. He took me back to Tanana after what I thought was a great vacation. Although I never did carry a fur-covered seat cover for the outdoor privies, I never forgot the need for one.

Another time I was in Huslia in mid-summer for a full clinic. Just as we were getting all of our medical supplies and the X-ray machine set up, two men rushed into the schoolhouse where we were planning to start seeing everyone.

"Doctor, can you come with us quickly," said one of the men. "My wife is so sick. She is in much pain. Please come."

"Of course, I'll come," I replied. Grabbing my bag, I followed the men. They went down to the river. There was a boat tied up to a log on the bank. We all got in and one of them started the motor.

It took about twenty minutes to reach their fish camp. We all jumped out and walked rapidly to the small cabin. In the bedroom was a young woman of about thirty lying in the bed moaning softly. Her children were standing by the bed crying. Two older women were standing close by.

I looked at her carefully. When I felt her forehead, it was easy to tell that her fever was high. Her abdomen was markedly distended. As I was pulling my stethoscope out of my bag, she looked at me and said, "I have to hang my clothes out on the line." With that, her head rolled to the side. She was dead. And I had been able to do nothing for her. Her diagnosis could have been any number of problems from intestinal obstruction or torsion on the bowel, to an ectopic pregnancy, or a ruptured appendix. We would never know.

After getting all the information about her that I could from her husband, I picked up my bag and again followed the path down to the river. Soon I was back in Huslia, with all the villagers lined up, waiting to be seen, along with their aching teeth to be pulled. The working day had just begun.

THE LITTLE BOY IN BETTLES

April is a time of "break-up" when all the ice in Alaskan rivers crack and separate into great hunks crashing together in tremendous thunderous noise. Just after the Yukon River break-up in 1954, I went north with Hansen for a field trip to Bettles (pop.75) further up in the Interior of this wild land, Bettles is way up on the Koyukuk River, 120 miles north of Tanana and 125 miles from Fairbanks.

This time I took my head nurse, Dorothy Bennett, with me. She was bright, a hard worker, an excellent organizer and a lot of fun. I was happy to have her with me. She was tall, slender, had red hair and a temper to match, which, fortunately, rarely was displayed. This was her first trip with me because generally she ran the hospital when I was away on a trip to the villages. This time we had a capable nurse who could substitute for her.

Dorothy took care of gathering all the medical supplies, including examining tools, a variety of medications, and even an emergency kit in the event of an unexpected delivery. These were put into pillowcases that were easily squashed into the back of Hansen's four-seater plane. This time there would be no X-ray machine taken because we had taken all the chest X-rays on a previous trip. We already knew all those who had active tuberculosis, all of whom were on the waiting list for a bed in the Mt. Edgecomb hospital, the Anchorage ANS hospital or in one of several sanatoriums in Washington State. While the patients waited, we isolated them in a separate part of their homes to prevent the spread of the disease to other members of the family. This was not a good solution, but better than none.

When we landed in Bettles about 10 a.m., we could see that there was lots of clear water in the river with very few chunks of ice. Evidently the Koyukuk River had had an earlier than usual break-up for this more northcentral part of Alaska. The land had been soaked with rain, which was obvious by the mud-coated boots of everyone coming toward our plane. When we climbed out of the plane and walked past the edge of the gravel airstrip, we sank almost knee deep into the mud and standing water. Fortunately, we had worn high rubber boots reaching close to our knees. Close by the airstrip, but still in the mud, was an encampment of Coast and Geodetic Survey men, those stalwart outdoorsmen who surveyed the land all over the 500,000 square miles of Alaska, which is twice the size of Texas. Their tents were all staked in the mud. Close by, on the end of the airstrip, were several helicopters that they needed for their work. The mud did not seem to bother the men as they waded through the mud smiling happily, apparently quite delighted to see us, a bit of diversion for them. They had apparently been out in the Bush for several months and were obviously lonesome. They offered to help us in any way they could, even suggesting we go for a ride in one of their helicopters. We thanked them kindly, but we had to go to work. There was so much to do.

Bettles was separated into two sections. We had landed in the CAA area. Andy Anderson who worked for Wein Airlines was the only pilot in Bettles. He and his wife Hannah lived, owned, and ran the roadhouse in that part of Bettles. Andy had built the roadhouse himself when he had come to Bettles to live a few years earlier. The other part of Bettles was five miles down river where most of the Native people lived as well as a white trader and his wife. The traders had some rooms available for overnight visitors above the store, which we would occupy when we arrived.

We started the first part of the clinic in one of the CAA buildings. No sooner had we set things up than a young mother came in carrying her eight-year-old son.

"Doctor, he was chopping wood and he put the axe right through his foot," she said anxiously.

"Okay, let me have a look at him," I replied. She put him down on a chair and the little boy held out his right foot, covered with blood, still dripping. Sure enough, he had put the axe right through the middle of his foot. Oh, so lucky, he had missed the bones and most of the blood vessels. After a careful examination to be sure there were no fractures or other major problems, I sutured his foot, first the top, then turned it over and sutured the bottom. After using lots of pressure and bandaging we put him in a chair with his foot up, where we could keep an eye on him. Not once had he uttered a cry. This was typical of the Native people in general who are amazingly stoic as I found through all the years I worked with them. The youngster remained content watching us work until the clinic was over. After that he hopped up on my back and I carried him piggyback for the rest of the morning.

After having lunch at the roadhouse, we repacked our medical supplies to go down river to check the rest of the people there. There were no roads to the Native part of Bettles which was five miles from the rest of the village. In fact there were no roads between any of my villages. This time preceded the advent of snowmobiles. We were hoping to get one of the men to give us a ride in one of the boats since there was only an occasional piece of ice in the river. Luckily, one of the CAA men by the name of Jim Falls came over.

"I'll take you, Doctor, whenever you are ready to go," he said.

"We accept, with pleasure," I replied.

Jim was a tall, lean, taciturn young man of Norwegian descent, very handsome as well. When we were in the boat he made quite a picture as he sat by the motor piloting us down river. His hair was blond, his jaw rugged, and he was dressed in a red plaid shirt, jeans and a cap, with the ear flaps down to keep his head warm. He was the perfect picture of the tough but warm-hearted Alaskan individual. All over Alaska we found that both Natives and white men were always eager with offers to help whenever there was a need. Jim was all business though, and quickly pulled the rope to start the engine. Once started he never spoke a word, not until he had to later on our journey.

We had on medium-weight jackets over which we had put the necessary life jackets. It was a warm and sunny April day. Light-heartedly, Dorothy and I had gotten in the boat, joined by George from the Coast and Geodetic group who seemed quite taken with Dorothy. The "boys" had piled our medically loaded pillowcases in behind us and we headed out into the river where we now noted a few pieces of ice floating by, leftovers we thought from the early break-up.

All went well for a short while, until suddenly the river was filled with ice chunks of all sizes rushing by us, some three and four times the size of our own boat, which was literally surrounded by them. We figured that an ice jam in the river above the village must have broken loose. The ice was crowding us more and more, and we suddenly realized we were in a very dangerous situation. We became very quiet for a few moments because we knew that if we capsized, there would be little chance of survival even with our life jackets on. We would freeze in that icy water and would likely be crushed between the ice chunks, which were even much larger below the water. We didn't have time to be afraid though, because we became very busy. Jim fought with the motor trying to keep it going long enough to get us to shore while George, Dorothy, and I tried to shove the ice aside with the oars or our hands. Then the motor quit! The propeller was crushed, and we were not sure if the boat would hold out. Slowly, with tremendous effort, we managed to push away some of the larger chunks of ice from the left side of the boat and gradually, very gradually; we were able to reach the riverbank. We jumped out into the water to beach the boat.

Of all the places we could have reached, ours was the best. We had a partially sandy beach covered with logs and branches. We cleared the beach fairly quickly by gathering up a huge pile of the wood. Most of this was nice and dry, since it was under the over-hanging banks, and there were plenty of small branches for kindling. The matches in our jackets were dry, so soon we had a roaring fire. We needed this because we had almost frozen our legs wading ashore in that icy water, in spite of our rubber boots which kept our feet dry. We had made a big mistake by not dressing warmly enough for travel in the Bush. We certainly had not planned on a detour like this. But any river water, even in the summer, is so cold that it is a rare individual who can survive in the water more than a few moments. Our jackets had not protected us enough, so the warmth of the fire felt like heaven. Though we should have worn warmer clothes there was no way that we could have known about the ice jam up river.

It was only after we were safe on solid ground on the riverbank did we begin to shake, realizing that we had all nearly been crushed to death.

Our next problem was to figure out how we were going to get ourselves out of our predicament. In those days there were no GPS units, no cell phones, not even regular phones in the Bush. No one carried two-way radios. We had no way of communicating, and certainly no one else was going to be crazy enough to go out in their boats with all the ice in the river. Obviously, rescue by water was not going to be an option. We just had to hope that the smoke from our fire might alert someone flying by to our plight.

As soon as the fire warmed us up, we all noted a very empty spot in our stomachs. We were hungry. All that exercise and the tension from the river part of our venture was taking its toll. As usual, I did have two candy bars in my pocket and Jim Falls had a few crackers in his. We shared these with the others. They helped but were not overly satisfying. So, we sat on a log by the fire and talked and talked. That is, Dorothy and I talked, with an occasional comment from our intrepid friends. The wind began to blow, which did not add to our comfort.

While we had hoped someone might see the smoke from our fire as a signal that we were stranded, no one did, but the trader down river decided that it was getting late, so he put in a call by radio to the CAA in Bettles to see when we were coming down. That is when he learned we had left on Jim's boat with George over three hours before. Since the distance between the two sections of the village was so close, the obvious conclusion was that something had happened to us. The biggest concern was that our boat had overturned and that we all had been crushed by the ice.

Right away one of the Coast and Geodetic Survey pilots took off to look for us in his helicopter. By this time, we had cleared quite a large space on the beach by burning so much of the wood. We heard the burr of the helicopter motor as it headed our way. We jumped up, waved our jackets and yelled, though the motor drowned our voices out. The pilot saw us, circled, banked, and the next thing we knew he was landing right beside us. We clambered into the helicopter, with all our gear, and were in the air within three minutes. He ferried us down to the main part of the village where most of the Native people lived. Thus, we had our helicopter ride after all. We arrived at about 6 p.m. and were greeted warmly by everyone there. We were then whisked to the traders' home where we had a wonderful dinner of moose meat, with some of their own vegetables, tomatoes and beans grown in the garden back of the store. Some of the most fertile garden plots are found in Bush Alaska, much to the surprise of "Outsiders," because the soil is so rich and the summer sunlight lasts twenty-four hours a day. In parts of Alaska, some of the vegetables are the largest grown in all of the USA. In the MatSu Valley, thirty miles north of Anchorage, some of the cabbages are mountainous in size reaching a hundred pounds.

By the time we finished dinner it was late in the evening and the clinic was put off until morning since no one in the village was acutely ill. Bed in their upstairs rooms that night was preferable and soon we were asleep. The rooms were rustic with no amenities other than the nice warm quilts on the beds. There was no TV, this being the time before the advent of television in the villages. There was no radio in the room. For lighting there was one light bulb hanging from the ceiling in the middle of the room. On a table was a basin with a jug of water and towels beside it. This was for our wash-ups. By the window was a rope ladder in case of fire. At 10 p.m., like it or not, the light would go out. That was the time the trader turned off his generator that supplied the electricity for the house.

As for other necessary facilities, there was an outhouse or, if one was not too sensitive to odors, a small back room with a honey bucket, emptied daily by one of the little boys in the village.

In the morning Dorothy and I set up our supplies on a long table in the store and then we held our regular clinic, seeing almost everyone in the village, removing teeth as necessary, but not as many as on previous visits. Sanitation was always a problem but we had a large bottle of alcohol and we did the best we could with that and a small basin with soapy water, also boiling any instruments that we might need on the stove.

One of the major complaints the Natives had on our field trips was "toothache," and since it was a rare occasion for a dentist to travel to the villages we had to deal with the dental complaints in our clinics. Teeth had not been much of a problem prior to the arrival of the white traders who set up shop bringing soft drinks and candy to the villages. The kids, of course, preferred these treats to their healthy Native diet, and huge holes in the teeth followed with resultant pain. We had no equipment to fill teeth so extraction was the only relief. We used a combination of Novocain with ephedrine that I injected, hopefully hitting the right nerve for the tooth in question to be pulled. Most of the time the injection worked. Dental education was given but the kids were not impressed and just grinned when they heard it.

There were no major medical problems in the village, much to our relief, so after a good visit with everyone, the same Coast and Geodetic Survey pilot who had rescued us the day before, flew down to pick us up. No sooner had we landed in the CAA area of Bettles than the little boy with the injured foot came hopping down on one foot to meet us on some borrowed crutches, which he flung aside as soon as he was close to us. He climbed up on my back to continue his piggyback ride.

There he remained until we left Bettles, save for the time I put him down long enough to redress his foot. There was no sign of infection, nor did he have any problems with his foot after he was checked by a local volunteer who removed his sutures five days later.

After that, Andy's little daughter, Mary Eva, took up riding piggyback on her mother's back. A new fad was started in Bettles. After lunch at the roadhouse, we flew back home to Tanana, this time with Andy in his Beaver, a somewhat larger plane than Hansen's Piper.

It was good to be back home in Tanana, although the near-death adventure on the Koyukuk River remained heavily on our minds. It made us realize how close we had come to death, which is a constant reality in all Bush living. Thankful we were to the Coast and Geodetic Survey pilot who had rescued us, as well as for the little boy's stoicism during the repair of his foot injury. But most of all, I missed his closeness on my back.

Hannah and Mary Eva Anderson and Jean with the little eight-year-old boy who had put his axe through his foot.

Coast & Geodetic field survey unit with helicopters, Bettles

Jim Falls steering us down the Koyukuk River to Bettles village in his motor boat, April 1954

George fending off the ice on our trip down to Bettles village, 1954

Caught in break-up ice as we headed down the Koyukuk River to Bettles Village, 1954

Coast and Geodetic helicopter flying in to rescue us when we were stranded on the beach of the Koyukuk River

After landing on the Bettles airfield, Dorothy Bennett and Jean were given a truck ride to the Wien lodge by the Coast and Geodetic men

Spring mud in Bettles village

Dog team housing in Bettles village

RESCUE

When the snow was still real deep in mid-April of 1954, we got a message from the CAA. The sun was bright because spring was in full force, although the temperature was in the upper twenties.

Hospital rounds had been completed followed by a short clinic when a message arrived from the airfield. A plane was overdue.

"Oh my gosh," I said. This was the first flight that I had arranged with Cy Hetherington who had just gotten his commercial license. He had had many hours of private flying and was an accomplished pilot, so I had not hesitated to hire him when a Public Health nurse in Kaltag needed to get to Fairbanks with a baby who needed to come to Tanana.

Cy had left Tanana earlier in the day for Kaltag and had notified the CAA when he left Kaltag about noon. It was now about four p.m., long past the time he should have reached Tanana. Right away I went down to Hansen's trailer. Luckily he had decided not to go hunting. He hurried down to the field to gas up his Piper Family Cruiser. My head nurse Dorothy wanted to go on the search for Cy, too, and since the added eyes would be invaluable, we both put on all our warm gear: parkas, boots and mitts. We also took a bunch of medical supplies, which we carried in the usual pillowcase that fitted well into the back of the plane. By 4 p.m. we were ready and Hansen took off on skis from the short snow-covered field.

Our route took us over the still-frozen Yukon River that was heavily laden with snow. It was easy to follow the usual course over the river heading down-river toward Kaltag.

About forty-five minutes into the flight we spotted the crash site. Cy was standing by the demolished red plane, waving his arms as we flew over. Hansen banked his plane sharply, making a one-eighty turn, and then made a soft landing on the deep spring snow, which flew up over our windshield as we came to a fairly rapid stop. He landed as close to Cy's plane as he could.

As rapidly as we could, Dorothy, Hansen, and I made our way through the snow, which was up to our hips, so the going was slow. "Are you hurt?" was our first question.

"No," replied Cy, "but the nurse is complaining about her back and the baby is crying."

Quickly we checked the baby, who luckily was in good shape except for a chipped tooth. The nurse had pain in the middle of her back whenever she moved. This, we found later, to be caused by several compressed vertebrae. Without a stretcher it was not easy to get the nurse out of the crashed plane, but we managed, using a blanket pulled taut as a stretcher, along with the help of a pair of snowshoes that Hansen had in his emergency equipment.

We slid her out of Cy's plane carefully, protecting her back as best we could and pulled her slowly over the slightly crusted snow to Hansen's plane. We got her settled flat in his plane by taking out the right front seat. With the seat out, she was able to lie relatively comfortably, as long as she didn't move. Fortunately she was a small woman, so fit well in the plane. A few of the pain pills that I had in my supplies worked wonders for her and she soon fell asleep, wrapped warmly in several blankets.

Then Dorothy carried the baby over as well. The baby was so good. After the first shock of the crash the baby never uttered another cry. Dorothy took care of both of them while I rotated between the two planes. Cy didn't want to leave his plane so he stayed by the remnants. Even if he had wanted to join the others there was no more room for him in Hansen's plane. Cy was a big man, six feet one and over two hundred pounds.

In walking between the two planes, I lost my warm, soft, sheepkin liners and mukluks in the deep snow that went up to the top of my hips. I got these liners and mukluks a while ago when I was on a trip to Anaktuvak Pass. Losing them left me walking back and forth in my just my heavy wool socks. I was so busy I gave no thought to the possibility of frostbite.

Hansen climbed into his plane and called in to advise the CAA that we had found the crash, that no one was in acute distress but he had no way to get us out because the snow was too deep to take off. He was able to give the CAA our exact location on the Yukon River. The CAA then reported to Eielson Air Force Base in Fairbanks that we had a problem and needed help. They had a brand new large, very heavy rescue helicopter that would be sent down-river to rescue us.

86

It would be the first rescue trip that this new model helicopter would make. We were excited to know that soon help would come.

After all that work we were hungry, but somehow Hansen did not have his emergency food supply on board, nor did I have my own emergency supply of candy bars with me.

Within the hour we heard the drone of an airplane that came closer and closer. It was a C-47 that Eielson had sent out to locate us. It circled and circled over us. We waved happily, but of course there was no way it could land on the river.

What the pilot did do was to get low enough for one of his men to throw down supplies to us out of the door. Down came flashlights, a two-way radio so we could talk to the pilot, some food, matches along with enough kindling and wood to make a small fire, chocolate, crackers, and soup. All this plus three thick, warm blankets and two walkie-talkies so we could talk between the planes on the ground. That made us all feel better, as did the news that the helicopter was coming very soon to pick us up.

After almost an hour we heard something that sounded like the motor of a helicopter. As it got louder and louder the snow began to fall. By now it was about 11 p.m. and very dark. The two-way radio made some noise. The pilot said he knew where we were but he couldn't come any closer because of increasing snow. He would go back to Tanana and wait there until the weather cleared, then make another trip down. The sound of the helicopter got fainter and fainter until it disappeared entirely. The snow fell thicker and thicker. This was a bit discouraging, but the nurse and the baby were warm and dry with Dorothy in Hansen's plane. We had all eaten some soup, crackers, and chocolate so were no longer hungry.

Hansen, Cy, and I were a little cold since we were camped out under Cy's remaining wing for a little shelter, still getting our exercise by going back and forth frequently between the two planes, which were about sixty feet apart. My feet, oddly enough, did get cold but were not freezing, thanks to the double-thick wool socks that I had ordered from Sears months before. They were well worth the extra price I had paid for them. I can't believe how warm my feet stayed in those wool socks. My wonderful soft sheepskin liners and mukluks were never found.

We kept busy heating up cocoa and making soup with the small fire we had made, but not too close to Cy's plane for fear of a major fire and explosion. About an hour later we heard the helicopter making another try, but as it got closer the snow again started coming down heavily, and again the pilot radioed that he had to go back.

Finally on the third attempt, about 4 a.m. the 'copter got through. Because of the danger of the helicopter, large and heavy as it was, of going through the ice, the pilot did not land but barely touched the snow and hovered above it. Quickly the medic jumped out bringing with him a stretcher for the nurse. We got her aboard the helicopter rapidly with the baby and Dorothy. At first the pilot said he could not take the rest of us because of the excess weight, but then he said I could come aboard, too. Then at the last minute, he okayed Cy.

We were all in the helicopter within ten minutes, and off we flew with the nurse well- secured on a real stretcher. Dorothy held the baby. Cy was strapped in, then the medic told me to take off my pants because my lined jeans were caked solidly with ice and snow. He was worried about frostbite. He did give me a blanket to wrap up in.

By now it was thirty minutes past four in the morning and we were all exhausted but happy. Just before the landing in Tanana the medic told me I'd better put my pants on and even suggested that I comb my hair because there would be photographers when we landed. Sure enough, the newspapers in Fairbanks had been alerted about the rescue mission by the Air Force, chiefly because this was the first mission that the new rescue helicopter had been called on. Even at this ungodly hour, the reporters had flown in from Fairbanks to cover the emergency rescue.

As we got off the helicopter, lights flashed in our eyes and I was glad to have on my pants.

The nurse was flown on into Fairbanks to be hospitalized in the old St. Joe's Hospital. Cy, Dorothy, the baby, and I were happy to be back in Tanana.

After the large helicopter had taken off from the Yukon River crash site, even without the great lights from the helicopter, Hansen had managed to stomp down enough snow to make a short field. He then dug his skis loose from the snow and ice that had formed around them. Without any additional weight in the plane and with a makeshift runway, he was able to get up in the air. So he came home to Tanana that morning, too.

I visited the nurse in Fairbanks a week later. She, too, did very well after the harrowing experience of the crash. Cy went home to Fairbanks a few days later, and the baby went back to Kaltag with no problems. All is well that ends well.

Many years later, when discussing the reasons for Cy's plane crash, his son, Tom Hetherington, told me that Cy had wrecked the plane while attempting to land on the Yukon River near Kokrines during white-out conditions in a spring snow storm. He had planned to land on the river and sit out the storm, but crashed when he was unable to see anything. The plane was a Stinson 108. To quote Tom, "It was a miracle that anyone made it out alive. The tubular construction of the Stinson saved them, had it been an all aluminum-skinned Cessna, it would have burned and all would have died."

Hansen by Cy Hetherington's crashed Stinson on the Yukon River, April, 1955

*Cy Hetherington standing by the remains of his crashed Stinson,
lucky to be alive, 1955*

New Air Rescue Helicopter from U.S. Army, Fairbanks

Toughy

Letter to my Brother

1/27/1954
Tanana, Alaska

Dear Stan:

I write you this, whether or not you show it to Poppa, you decide.

It all started at 5 p.m. yesterday as far as we were concerned. The phone between the CAA and the hospital rang for me as I was going into supper, with a message. Toughy Edgington, a gold miner downriver, had cracked up (in his plane). Would I go? Of course. The CAA manager then came down with a note. The crash was close to Kallands, 30 miles downriver, and the note begged for help—Toughy, with both ankles broken and bleeding badly, his wife who was about five months pregnant, and a Native passenger who was cut up a good deal.

It was already dark and the chances of a plane getting in before morning were very slim. Kallands is composed of three or four cabins and that is all. So, one of our boys, Basco Minook, quickly got all the dogs he could find and hitched them up to his sled.

I ate hastily and then dressed warmly—three pairs of pants (the outside ones the heavy army arctic type), three sweaters, parka, three pairs of wool socks, mukluks with the sheep-skin lining and fur mitts. Basco dressed similarly.

The nurses packed up medical supplies, including three bottles of IV fluids. Someone handed me a .38 cal. pistol in case of wolves. Of course I didn't know how to shoot with it. Hopefully Basco could. I stuck it in my pocket and put the IV fluids between my legs so they wouldn't freeze. Someone else threw a couple of wool blankets over me. The rest of the supplies were thrown into the sled and off we went. I left a message for a plane to pick up some plasma in Fairbanks and drop this and leg splints if and when a plane could get down to the crash site. It was dark, the weather a bit brisk, forty below when we started and fifty below by the time we reached there. Basco yelled and cussed, mostly running behind the sled, the dogs were too slow when he rode. We mushed along. It was hard to see the trail and there were many large ice cracks, eight to twelve inches wide.

The first time the sled turned over, Basco's leg went into an ice crack up to his hip. For a few minutes we thought he had broken it, but it was just a good wrench. We continued mushing along. Each time we'd turn over he'd pick me up along with the sled, and right us up together. Seventeen miles we went down to "Old Station," a one-cabin spot. Here, the Natives had gotten the message about our trip on the radio. Another team, this one well-trained, was ready to take me on. We warmed up by the fire while the medical supplies were being put on the new sled.

Then, after bidding Basco good-bye, with my new musher, Joe John Nicholi, I took off for the last thirteen miles. His dogs were excellent, our only trouble being that it was so dark we couldn't see and every now and then Joe John would take the flashlight to find the trail. When the Yukon River froze up, it had big ice hunks sticking up all over, not like some of the smaller rivers. When we would get off the trail, the traveling was a bit rough. I still suggest foam-rubber cushioning for all dog-sled passengers.

We started our journey from Tanana at a quarter of six. We reached Kallands at 12:30 a.m. and found that a plane had gotten through, after all. Bob Byers, a very fine Bush pilot, one of the best, had risked a landing and most unbelievably, had made it. He met us, pulled me out of the sled, and we climbed up the steep hill to the cabin.

A quick survey showed Toughy conscious, but in severe pain with a four-inch cut to his forehead, a deep and long cut on his neck extending up to his chin, a badly swollen right hand (X-ray later showed two fractures in this), a broken right ankle and a compound fracture of the left ankle. At a glance, the other two looked as though they could wait, so I went right to work on Toughy, first giving him a big shot of morphine, starting an IV, using the plasma that Bob Byers had brought with him from Fairbanks.

As soon as Toughy was feeling a little better, I checked on the other two. I had gone down prepared to deliver a premature, but Toughy's wife Roz was still holding on to the baby and otherwise Roz had just had one tooth knocked out. The other passenger, Lottie Justin, about sixty years old, had a deep laceration of the forehead. The crash had occurred the night before, just as Toughy was taking off. The three stayed all night alone. By morning, Lottie said she could stand it no longer and she walked eight miles at forty below to the nearest cabin for help. She found Bobby Swenson with a dog team and she gave him a note to bring to us. He had a crack team and made the 30-mile trek in four hours. That's how we were notified to get started.

Toughy had tried to take off in his plane, couldn't gain altitude, and went down. He was in the pilot's seat, the women were in the back. The plane was demolished.

Toughy's chest was squashed into the steering wheel and his feet were all tangled up in the foot controls. Roz and Lottie worked for an hour and a half getting him out. Roz literally pulled the metal bars apart with her hands to get him out of the plane. The two women managed to pull him up the steep hill to the top of the hill. Toughy is big—240-250 pounds. When they reached the top of the hill, he crawled on his hands and knees with his two broken ankles to the cabin, and there they all stayed until we got there. Brave people, these three, and tough. They found firewood in the cabin and matches, so, with a nice fire going, soon were warm, though Toughy was in shock. Somehow, they had been able to get him onto a cot, then covered him with blankets that were in the cabin. When we arrived I could barely get a blood pressure on him at first, but the IV fluids made a big difference, as did the morphine that I had brought with me. We were all busy.

Bob Byers, after things got under control, took Roz and Lottie on to Tanana Hospital while I worked on Toughy. Bob brought back two CAA men to help carry Toughy to the plane. We had him splinted, doped up, and revived by the plasma, plus multiple doses of the morphine.

They made a stretcher with poles and a piece of canvas, and we (Bob, the CAA men, and I) carried him down the hill on the slippery, icy, narrow path with hairpin curves to the plane. How the men were able to get him into the plane, a small Cessna, I still find hard to fathom. Then I crawled in and sat by Toughy on a sack, keeping his IV going, while Bob took off. By now, it was after 5 a.m. We reached Fairbanks at 7 a.m., but due to the thick ice fog, we couldn't land, so Bob circled and circled until we almost ran out of gas, and then he had to land.

I had been beginning to wonder how much longer the gas would hold out, when a sudden breeze sprang up, and the field cleared. An ambulance was waiting. I gave Toughy one more shot of morphine to keep him from hurting too much on the rough dirt road leading to town. The ambulance driver helped us get him into the ambulance. Then he drove us carefully to St. Joseph's hospital. When we reached the hospital, I went in to get him admitted and to be sure the specialist was there. Dr. Hagland, the bone specialist, was already waiting for Toughy.

First X-rays. Poor Toughy, any movement killed him, but he took it all, holding fast to my hand with his swollen right hand. Then the X-rays showed two bones broken in this hand. We looked at the films, and Dr. Haglund explained what he would have to do and he took over Toughy's care. An hour later, the CAA called the hospital to say Bob Byers would take me home at 10:30 a.m.

After leaving Toughy in the hospital in the competent hands of Dr. Hagland, I walked over to the all night café to have a cup of coffee. I went into the café and dragged myself up on a stool at the counter. I was tired. After ordering some coffee and toast, I unzipped my parka, because the café was warm. As I did so, the large 20-cc syringe that I had used on Toughy fell out of my pocket onto the floor. Sitting at the café tables were a number of men having their morning coffee, who, upon seeing the syringe, gaped at me. Quickly I pulled my parka back, to put the syringe in a safer spot. As I did so, the .38 cal. revolver in my pants' pocket was quite visible. There was a gasp from the men. I got up, zipped up my parka, put a few coins on the counter, and left.

Finding a cab, I headed back to the airfield. I had to borrow ten dollars from Bob to pay the cabbie, because I never carried any money with me. It was a beautiful day. Bob Byers' plane had been gassed up and checked over. We headed for home. Roz, by this time, had flown on from Tanana to Fairbanks with Hansen to be with her husband. She still showed no signs of premature labor. Lottie stayed on in Tanana with us for a little while. Beside her head wound, she was shaken up pretty much in general. On our return to Tanana, I checked the hospital patients, took a hot bath, and slept all afternoon.

This evening, I've been listening to the radio reports about the crash. Toughy will be good as new in a couple of months, the baby's okay and still in Roz. All's well that ends well.

I'm sleepy, so think I'll hit the hay early tonight, will probably sleep in for a few hours in the morning. I have one baby due, but otherwise there should be no interruptions.

Good Night,

Love Jean

Addendum: The next week, when I went into Fairbanks to see Toughy, I found Bob Byers, in the bed next to him with a broken leg. He had been shoveling snow off of his roof and had fallen off. We had a good reunion.

An oil painting of Jean at rescue site by William "Rex" Rexrode, painted after the plane crash and rescue trip. Rex was a good friend who had a talent for painting. This was a treasured gift and is displayed prominently in Jean's home today.

Baby on the Wing

One late winter day in February of 1954, several hours after the regular scheduled radio call, the CAA sent a messenger down to the hospital with a message from Father Baud, the Catholic priest in Nulato.

One of Father Baud's parishioners who was in the late stages of pregnancy had begun to bleed heavily. The neighbor who acted as midwife was very worried, so he called the CAA, who relayed the information down to me at the hospital. Considering the risk for this woman, I knew I had better get down to the village as soon as possible. Unfortunately, the distance was over a hundred miles away, so after receiving the message, I hurried down the road to Garfield Hansen's trailer to see if Hansen was available to fly me to Nulato, which was well over an hour's flight away. Fortunately, he was in his trailer.

As soon as we knew that Hansen was available, my head nurse Dorothy started to pack up the all the necessary medical supplies at the hospital, including some IV fluids that might be needed to care for the Native woman in distress. All of the supplies were stuffed into a pillowcase, which was the only way we could get them to fit safely in the back of the four-seat Piper. The plane had only a minimal amount of packing space, because the rest was always filled with emergency gear: the tent, food, and sleeping bags in case the plane went down.

Although it was dark already, the weather was clear so the Yukon River was easy to follow down to Nulato. The temperature was moderately cold, only about twenty to twenty-five degrees below zero. Hansen's heating area up in the front of the plane gave off almost no heat, so we had dressed warmly with our parkas, boots and heavy mitts.

After landing on the short dirt airstrip on top of the hill above Nulato, we were met by Father Baud and several of the villagers. They greeted us with a wheel barrow into which we quickly placed our heavy pillow case with the medical supplies, then they led us down the narrow, curving, icy path to the village below, Hansen coming with us as he always did in case his help was needed.

Into my patient's log cabin I went. It was warm and cozy with a wood stove radiating heat from the center of the main room. The family's four other children stood quietly in the corner of the room, sensing that all was not well with their mother. My patient's bleeding had slowed down somewhat but was still a worry. Her contractions had stopped which was a good sign, but the concern was over a possible abnormally placed placenta that might have started to tear away from the lining of the womb.

After the children were sent out of the room, a brief exam revealed that the head was barely engaged, i.e. the head was just starting down the birth canal. She was minimally dilated and very little fresh blood was present. So, she, her husband, the midwife, and I had a brief conference. We could stay there for the delivery or go back to Tanana where we would be better-equipped should major problems develop. Because of the bleeding, the risks were considerable. After the few minutes' discussion, we decided it would be better to go back to the hospital. Some of the men brought a stretcher from Father Baud's storage area, covering her with a wool blanket to carry her up the hill.

To make enough room for her in the plane, Hansen removed the right front seat and the left rear seat, leaving the right rear seat for my patient and the pilot's seat so he could fly the plane. Thus, we got in, with me behind Hansen, crouching over next to my patient in the back. She sat on her seat uncomfortably but with her legs outstretched.

Off we flew in the cold and dark. All was well until we were about thirty minutes out from Tanana. The plane felt as though it had hit a bump, then it dropped suddenly about 500 feet. There was a touch on my shoulder. "Doctor, it's coming." Sure enough, the baby's head was crowning. There was no overhead light in the plane, but bashful Hansen held a flashlight in his right hand. He would not turn his head to see if the light were on the right area so I had to turn his arm and hand so the light would fall in the proper place. The delivery was awkward with me in contortions trying to ease the baby out within the tiny space available. However, all went well until I needed the scissors to cut the cord.

Nowhere, as I dug into the pillowcase behind me, could I find the scissors. Ever helpful Hansen pulled his penknife out of his pocket, opened it and handed it to me. Not exactly sterile, but I did wipe it off with a little alcohol before cutting the cord, then tied the cord with a small piece of string. I wrapped the baby girl in the blanket that Hansen had tried to warm in front of the plane's tiny heater. Quickly, I slipped off my parka to wrap around the baby who, by this time, was squalling away at the top of her lungs. What a great sign that was. The baby girl really objected to her arrival in the bitter cold, black night, high up in the air. I had to keep checking her to be sure she did not slide out of the parka. Luckily, the placenta came out easily. It was at least thirty below zero outside the plane by this time, and not much warmer inside the plane. My stoic patient held the vials with the medications so I could fill the syringe to give her an injection to help the uterus contract.

Hansen never once looked back. He had called Tanana to let them know that we would be landing soon, so the old black hospital pickup truck, all warmed up, was there waiting at the end of the field to meet us. I did not give any thought until way later to that horrific mess in the plane, all that blood and amniotic fluid. It was Hansen who went back the next morning to thaw out the cabin with a heater and clean everything up, not an easy task at -30º F without a hanger. He was quite a guy.

The baby was named Josephine Jean, partly for her airborne de-livery somewhere between Kokrines and Tanana, partly after me. Had she been a boy, she would have been named Garfield after Hansen. Josephine Jean sounded a lot prettier. She grew up into a beautiful woman.

Somehow, the story about Josephine Jean was picked up from the Fairbanks newspaper and it was circulated all over the USA. Shortly thereafter, I began receiving penknives from all over the country, over seventy-five in all. The one I treasured the most was from the Surgeon General of the Public Health Service.

Lady Doctor, Pilot Deliver Baby in Sky

FAIRBANKS, Alaska, March 22. (UP) — A woman doctor, aided by an Alaska bush pilot, delivered a baby girl for a native woman in an airplane high over the Yukon River.

The baby was born in the back seat of a single-engined plane as Dr. Jean Persons and pilot Garfield Hansen assisted from the front seat. The mother, Mrs. Rita Pansy, had been taken aboard at Nulato for a flight to the Tanana Native Hospital.

Lacking a scissors to cut the umbilical cord, Dr. Persons said she borrowed pilot Hansen's pocket knife. She then wrapped the baby in her own coat and shivered in zero temperatures the last 30 minutes of the flight to Tanana.

Later, the baby was named "Josephine," for the song, "Come, Josephine, in My Flying Machine," popular several decades ago.

Dr. Persons is a niece of Maj. Gen. Wilton B. Persons, who is attached to President Eisenhower's staff at the White House.

The lady is probably out one coat! Don't you think? This in ATLANTA JOURNAL 3/21/55   Dad

"Outside" newspaper report, after baby delivered in Hansen's Piper Family Cruiser, 1954

HUGHES

A message was received from the CAA one evening in November. There was a little boy who lived in Hughes, a village on the Koyukuk River. He had a very high fever, a temperature of 105 degrees, and a stiff neck. Time was essential in getting to see and treat him because his diagnosis was most likely meningitis. This is a deadly disease.

After receiving the message from the CAA about the little boy, I went down the road to Hansen's place and knocked on his door. He opened his door. "Hansen, there is a very sick child in Hughes," I said. This was almost a hundred miles away up on the Koyukuk River. "Do you think you could fly me there to see him?"

By this time, the sky had darkened. He stepped out of his trailer to look up at the sky. After a few moments, he said, "Fifty-fifty chance we'll make it. Let's go." Hansen had not been in Tanana very long and had never been to Hughes before. I was a very trusting soul.

The nurse on duty quickly gathered my emergency supplies, stuffing them into the pillowcase that would fit into the back of Hansen's plane. This was a four-seater with over-size tires to make landing on the short bush airstrips easier.

Hansen went down to the field to gas up and to check the plane. The airstrip was about a mile down our one dirt road. The airstrip was short and unpaved but longer than the village airstrips.

Ambrose Kosevnikoff, our wonderful maintenance man, went and got the old black pickup, our only means of transportation for the hospital.

"Hi, Ambrose, thanks for your help."

"That's why I'm here Doc," he said, giving me his enormous smile.

I hopped into the front seat of the pickup with my full pillowcase. The pickup rattled as Ambrose drove to the field, despite the good care that Ambrose gave it. It was very old.

By the time we reached the field, Hansen was ready to go. The temperature was cool, not as cold as it had been. "Did you bring all your gear, Doc? I see you've got your warm things on."

"Yes," I replied, "and I hope you have yours." We both had

dressed warmly with our parkas, mitts, and I had some very warm boots with sheepskin lining that I had gotten from Anaktuvak Pass on a recent short trip there.

We always carried lots of gear when we flew in case we went down. Hansen supplied the tent, food, sleeping bags and all the basic emergency stuff. I always carried a couple of candy bars, a knife, matches, a comb and lipstick. I knew that if we had trouble any who would come to our rescue would have a camera. So I had to play it safe. The picture inevitably would end up not only in the local Alaska papers but Outside as well. How the stories got Outside I never knew.

Hansen took off easily in the dark. Because visibility was not great we followed the Yukon River until we reached the Koyukuk River. Here we turned north and headed for Hughes.

"Doc," said Hansen," I hope you don't mind going the longer way, but I don't think I can find Hughes unless we follow the river." He had none of the fancy equipment that almost all small planes have nowadays, just the turn and bank and the altimeter on his instrument panel.

"Whatever you think is the best way. You are the one who knows how to fly and I trust your judgment," I replied.

From here on the trip became quite hairy. The day had been fairly warm, now the cold air came down on the river and suddenly we were faced with such thick fog that almost all vision was occluded. Hansen descended until we were flying just above the river. Hansen had to literally skim over the river with its many bends as it turned and twisted.

It seems strange to me now, but on none of our flights while I lived in Tanana was I ever scared. Somehow, I knew we would always make it. All of the pilots that I flew with were highly skilled; except for the one I flew with once when he didn't have a door on my side. I had complete trust in them, despite our many trips. Now if I were to fly as I did then I would be petrified.

Following the river as we did made for a very slow flight, so it wasn't until about two in the morning that we found ourselves near Hughes. There was a low mountain just behind the village; which Hansen managed to skirt despite the dark. The houses were built right along the front of the river with a small cache behind each one. Of course it was too dark to see them but Patty James, who owned the local store along with her husband, had promised to have lights at each end of the field. As I recall the dirt field was only about nine hundred feet long. As we got closer, Hansen called in, "We are very close. Can you put the lights on?"

Almost immediately two lights shone down below us from two vehicles. Unfortunately, they were both at one end of the field. I held my breath but Hansen, somehow made the landing with no difficulty and I just said "Wow!"

The first thing we did was to greet Patty and Leslie James, the local traders. "How's the boy?" I asked.

"Not good," was the reply.

Hansen pulled the pillowcase with the medical supplies out from the back of the plane. "I'll carry them for you, Doc. You just go right on ahead."

"Okay, thanks," I replied and hurried on to the trader's home which doubled as a grocery store and post office. Patty had already taken the little boy with his mother to her place and the mother greeted us eagerly.

"Please Doctor, can you help?" The mother was so worried she was having trouble holding back tears.

A quick exam confirmed what we had believed when we first got our initial information back in Tanana. He did have meningitis. Hansen was right behind us and said, "Here are your supplies" and handed me the pillowcase. Our little patient did not shed a tear when I gave him an injection of antibiotics, followed by getting some fluids into him and then a cooling wash to help bring down his fever.

We stayed with him all-night, waiting until morning to take him back to Tanana. It would have been a grim flight with the fog had we tried to return that night. Hansen went over to the plane to gas up in the morning after eating the good breakfast Patty made for us. After that and another antibiotic injection, Hansen carried the boy to the plane and with his mother aboard with us we took off. The trip back was a direct flight because the fog had lifted and the skies were crystal clear. We made much better time in the air than on our way up. Before a week was up the little boy was fine, so he and his mother were able to return home to Hughes, happier and in better shape than the week before.

Patty and Leslie James, who was several years her senior, had lived in Hughes for a number of years. Together they ran the store, post office, and they showed three- reel movies in a warehouse- like building next door to their store. They lived on the second floor of the store and had a few extra rooms available for pilots and other visitors who flew into Hughes.

The 900-foot gravel airfield was very close to the few cabins on the left of the James' home. There were 55-gallon oil drums filled with gasoline for anyone who needed to fill the tanks. These drums were to be found on many of the airfields around the country. I have no idea who kept them filled since there were no roads between the villages and it never occurred to me to ask. They were invaluable to the small planes that often ran low on gasoline.

Patty was the one who really ran the grocery store. Leslie, her husband, was an old dear who accepted all of our teasing with great good humor. He had a terrific sense of humor. In the evenings we all sat around in their living room telling one story after another.

They had a son, Johnny, who, as I remember, must have been about twenty years of age. He did all sorts of jobs around the place to help his parents.

Then there was an adorable, but well spoiled little Native boy, named Timmy, for whom they were the official parents. Timmy had the run of the place and loved candy much too much, to the detriment of his teeth.

Prior to my arrival in Alaska, Patty and Leslie had adopted Timmy when he was a newborn. I saw his birth certificate signed by the physician who preceded me in Tanana. It seemed a puzzlement to me. It listed Patty as the birth mother and Leslie as the father, though Timmy really was the son of a lovely Native woman who lived in Hughes, a few cabins to the right of the store. She had a number of children and it was not uncommon in the villages for someone who had several children to let someone who did not have any children or maybe just one of their own to raise another's child. The child was loved by everyone and was accepted in everyone's home. No one seemed to object, so I did not try to make any changes. Timmy was welcome in his real mother's home and he played with his natural brothers and sisters whenever he wanted to. I must say his real brothers and sisters were much better behaved than he was.

Whenever we went to Hughes, to have clinic or just to visit, Timmy would grab my stethoscope and proceed to listen to the hearts of any and all who might be in the store. Most were willing subjects.

Hughes was a beautiful village, one of the most picturesque villages in my care. All the log houses lining the banks of the Koyukuk River were very well built and Hughes was one of the most attractive villages in my care. There were nothing out of place and the village was extremely neat. Each cabin had its own little log cache out back, built up high above the ground on stilts to protect the contents, mostly food, from the bears or other animals.

One evening in Tanana, the CAA sent a message down to the hospital to say that Patty James was very ill. She had chest pain and was vomiting. I went down to Hansen's trailer right away. It was dark already because it was fall. Why is it that emergencies in the villages seemed mostly to occur at night or when it was dark? They never seemed to occur as often when it was summer time when we had light all night long.

It didn't take long before we were in the air, headed for Hughes. By this time Hansen had been to Hughes a number of times so it wasn't nearly as an exciting flight as some of the other ones we had had before.

This time her son, Johnny, and her husband Leslie had lights at both ends of the short field; a big help.

We went right over to the store to see Patty, who, indeed was in dire straights. She had severe chest pain on the left side and she had acute tenderness in her abdomen in the right upper quadrant. She was running a fever and she was vomiting bile, that yucky yellow stuff.

After checking her over, I was not sure if she was having a heart attack or an acute gall bladder problem. Regardless, she had to get into Fairbanks immediately. I knew she would not survive if she remained in Hughes.

104

Hansen had gassed up almost as soon as we landed, expecting that we would be flying soon from the way Patty looked when we first saw her.

Leslie and Johnny fashioned a stretcher to carry her to the plane. Hansen took out the right front and back seats so the stretcher would fit. I crawled over her to sit by her side. By this time, I had given her morphine enough to cut her pain somewhat and had an IV started. Still, she was vomiting as we flew. However, the worst part of the trip was caused by the turbulence which developed as soon as we took off for Fairbanks. With each bounce, surging suddenly up, then suddenly down, Patty's pain and discomfort increased and it was difficult to control. We had no lights in the Piper Family Cruiser, so managing her pain and vomiting, and keeping the IV going was not easy. We had none of the nice IV catheters that are available nowadays.

Eventually, after the longest trip Hansen and I ever had from Hughes to Fairbanks, we landed. An ambulance that came responding to Hansen's radio call in to the CAA met us.

The CAA alerted St. Joseph's Hospital and we then made a quick and smooth ride to the hospital. Here I left Patty in the care of two excellent specialists, one an internist and the other a surgeon. Then back to Tanana Hansen and I flew.

The next day Bob Byers flew in from Fairbanks to Tanana with the mail and a message from the doctors at the hospital. Patty had had both a heart attack and an acute gall bladder attack. She had surgery for the latter, as soon as her heart was stabilized, and she returned to Hughes in three weeks where she went right to work at the store. She was a remarkable woman and a one very tough lady.

FATHER BAUD AND NULATO

Of all the people I worked with during my tour of duty at the ANS Hospital, one of my favorite individuals was Father Baud. He was a Frenchman, a Catholic priest, who after completing his seminary studies had been sent over directly from France to Alaska. He was a young man when he arrived in Alaska, though when I first met him in 1953 he must have been at least fifty years old. Except for a brief stop in Fairbanks to receive instructions from his Bishop, he was flown to his new home in the village of Nulato on the lower Yukon. There he had a church and a school where he and three nuns taught the Alaska Native children and cared for the rest of the villagers as well. There were at least forty children in the school of varying ages and classes from first through the eighth grades. After that, the children were sent down to the boarding school, Mt Edgecomb, in Southeast Alaska, many hundreds of miles from home.

Religion played a big part in the children's education and attendance at church services was strictly adhered to, though some of the children were not always in accord. Father Baud was busy all the time caring for his flock. He and the nuns were totally devoted to the children and to their work. Though the village was small with fewer than two hundred villagers there was little time for anything else other than their daily church devotions.

Father Baud was an artist of great talent. Many of his paintings were of his magnificent surroundings including the mighty Yukon River with the small outboard motor boats, all lined up on the river's edge. In the summer everything was green, but in the fall the leaves were turned in all shades of yellow on the many birch and aspen trees on the rolling hills making a breathless sight. One of my desires was to have one of his paintings. He promised me one but never had time to complete the painting he started for me.

While serving as the priest in Nulato, one of Father Baud's responsibilities was to stand by for the medical radio call that I held every afternoon at the Tanana Hospital with all the villages. Father Baud would have his list of the various illnesses or injuries of the villagers. As soon as I would call his radio call number he would answer promptly in his distinctive, rapid excited voice with his definite French accent.

Everyone who tuned into the same radio frequency up and down the river could easily recognize his voice.

When I had my regular three o'clock in the afternoon medical call to the villages, Nulato was one of the villages on my list. People up and down the river listened to this medical hour every day. It was part of the entertainment and sometimes it helped solve a problem for some one in one of the other villages. Most everyone knew everyone else, or at least knew of them, up and down the rivers, so it was one way of keeping in contact with the others. There was no such thing as our current Federal privacy acts.

Instead of his voice from Nulato, on a fall day in 1954, one of the nuns was on the radio with the information that Father Baud was having a nosebleed that they could not stop. I gave them some measures to stop the bleeding, but knew from what I heard that I needed to reach him as soon as possible. His bleeding sounded serious. It was then that I learned that he had a history of high blood pressure.

Hansen was in his trailer and was ready to fly. He and I rode down together to the field in the old, black pickup hospital truck. Very soon we were in the air for the flight to Nulato. As soon as we reached the village we found that some of the Native men had put Father Baud into the very same wheelbarrow that he always used to help carry our medical supplies down the hill to the village when we came to hold clinics. This time it was well padded with blankets with Father Baud as the occupant. In this manner he had been wheeled up the hill to the short airstrip. He was still bleeding, but by now it was slower, steady, no longer gushing.

He was rather pale, looking terribly frail, instead of his usual bouncy, energetic self. He was always thin, but now appeared tiny. After checking his blood pressure and starting an IV in his arm, with the bottle of fluid flowing, we got him into the plane by taking out the right front seat of the plane. I sat on his left side keeping the IV steady. I had tried to stop the bleeding by pressure then by using silver nitrate to cauterize the broken blood vessel, but neither attempt was successful.

Father Baud was in shock, with so much blood loss, but before we reached Fairbanks he was a bit more alert. An ambulance met us, thanks to Hansen's emergency call to the hospital. St. Joseph's' Hospital was ready and waiting for him, along with a specialist who was able to stop the bleeding.

Father Baud's blood pressure had stabilized somewhat since we had left Nulato, to a reasonable level. Phenobarbital was the drug I had given him before take off. In those days we had little to offer to treat blood pressure problems except for Phenobarbital.

After his admission to the hospital he had to have three blood transfusions. As soon as I knew Father Baud was out of danger and in the good hands of the specialist, I went back to the airfield where Hansen was waiting to take me back to Tanana.

Father Baud had a much-needed rest in Fairbanks and was able to go back to Nulato in about ten days, under strict mandate to slow down. Unfortunately he never took this recommendation from the Fairbanks doctor seriously, but somehow managed to survive until later when he was transferred to a town not far from Anchorage. There someone could keep an eye on him to keep him from overworking. Of course, by then he was quite elderly, at least up in his seventies.

Years later, when I was practicing in Anchorage, Sister Doris, one of the Nulato nuns, was transferred to Anchorage. She then became my patient. She was working way too hard with the prisoners to whom she had been assigned at the Correctional Facility out in Eagle River, but she, like Father Baud would not slow down. She still wore her nun's habit that for some reason pleased me. Nowadays it is hard to tell who is a nun and who is not.

About a year after her first visit with me, I diagnosed her with a fatal disease. At this point I transferred her care to that of my husband, Bob Whaley, who is an internist. He knew far more about caring for dying patients than I ever did. There was no cure for her but he was able, with a special pain cocktail, to keep her from suffering. The amount he gave her did not make her drowsy. She was able to think clearly, carry on a conversation with ease, even write notes to her friends before she died. I still have the one she wrote to me and treasure it. After she was hospitalized and during the end stages of her disease, I used to go visit her at Providence Hospital each day after I finished seeing the patients in my office, There, together, she in her bed, I in the chair beside her, we would talk and reminisce about the "old days."

We talked about her years in Nulato, about Father Baud, and about my visits to the village for clinics and emergencies. She had pictures of the little toddler from Ruby whom I had sutured back together after her severe dog mauling and scalping so many years before. She was now to be married. The pictures she had sent to Sister Doris showed a beautiful young woman, with not a scar visible on her face, despite her many lacerations from the sled dogs. Her hair hid the old scars on her scalp and somehow the facial ones had disappeared.

Memories of Nulato have remained with me all these years.

Once in a blue moon comes a man like Father Baud, devoted to his work with the children, his church, dedicated to all the villagers, never thinking of himself. He was someone I will always remember and feel so fortunate to have been able to know him.

* * * * * * * * *

Before I left Tanana in the summer of 1956, I had three field trips scheduled for villages down the Yukon River; Ruby, Galena, and Nulato. The time was March and the weather was a little unstable. Snow showers came and went. However, Hansen thought we could make the trip without difficulty, so he packed my nurse, all our gear, and me into his plane and we took off.

During the middle of the clinic in Ruby, a relatively small village, I developed some abdominal pain. We had planned to spend the nights in the first two villages, then fly home after we were through with Nulato, which was the furthermost village of the three from Tanana. I continued with the clinics in spite of the abdominal pain.

Each morning I checked with Hansen about his thoughts about the weather because my pain was increasing, plus the fact that I had started to run a fever. Galena was the largest village and took the longest time to be sure each villager was examined and treated, always with a number of teeth to be pulled. We then went on to Nulato.

Getting through the clinic in Nulato, which was the last village on our list was a bit harder, but Hansen, who knew by this time, that I was having some difficulty, assured me that the weather would hold and that he could get us to St. Joe's in Fairbanks when we were through. By the location of the pain and the fever I knew I most likely had a case of appendicitis. I restricted my intake to fluids just in case.

Hansen flew us home after everyone had been seen. He dropped off the nurse in Tanana along with the remaining medical supplies, then he gassed up and we were on our way to Fairbanks.

We got to Fairbanks and then to St. Joe's about eight in the evening. I refused to have the general surgeon operate on me. I didn't like him for some reason, but he was the only general surgeon in town. The Sisters then had to recruit the orthopedic surgeon who was the only other surgeon in Fairbanks. He nobly volunteered to do the surgery, but couldn't do it until morning.

One of my favorite Coast and Geodetic pilots, named Lee, whom I had met on one of my many trips to Hughes, was in Fairbanks. When he heard I was in the hospital he came right over to see me. Of all my friends he was the one who could make me laugh over absolutely nothing. I loved him dearly, as a special friend. When he came into my room he brought with him a bottle of a special cocktail that he had made, composed of some sort of juice and a bit of gin. All we did was tell stories and laugh until the wee hours.

The nurse who was supposed to be taking care of me was a brand new nurse and very young. She seemed to be scared of taking care of a doctor, so she gave us no problem, even though I was supposedly resting quietly. She would put a finger on her pursed lips, then leave. Why I had no problem from the delayed surgery I don't know, but I do know I suffered no pains that evening, maybe because I stayed on Lee's clear liquids.

The orthopedic surgeon gave me an incision that left me with a scar that later looked like railroad tracks, but I never did mind. One of the remarkable things about my hospitalization at St. Joe's was that when I got what I thought was my hospital bill a few weeks later in Tanana, all that was in the envelope was a note to say, "no charge", with an additional note that said thanks for taking care to my patients down river, and especially for taking care of Father Baud when he had his major emergency nose bleed. There is nothing better than to have friends in the right places.

Father Baud in front of the church in Nulato, 1953

The village of Nulato in winter, 1954

Salmon strips drying on racks by the Yukon River

Father Baud and two of the three nuns in Nulato

Graveyard on the hillside in Nulato

Fishwheels put up for winter on the bank of the Yukon River

ANAKTUVUK PASS

In July of 1953 I had a message from Bettles, way up on the Koyukuk River, to say that the people in Anaktuvuk Pass needed to have a clinic. They had had no doctor visit since the measles epidemic the year before. When no other doctor had been available, Dr. Stu Rabeau at Kotzebue had gone there to help. The measles epidemic had been ferocious. The Eskimos in the village of Anaktuvuk were the most nomadic of all the tribes in Alaska and had never been exposed to measles before. They had acquired no immunity to the disease. Also, there was no measles vaccine available in the early '50s.

The Eskimos were hit with the childhood disease because of a transient visitor with measles who had come through the village. Many were severely ill and many died. Oddly enough, more of the male population died than the women.

Hansen flew me up to Bettles from Tanana with a nurse and all my medical supplies. Here I met Andy Anderson who had been flying in the Arctic for years, so he flew me on up to Anaktuvuk Pass. As did all my pilots, he stayed with me to help in every way he could. He even had arranged for me to use the old military Quonset hut for the clinic.

My first trip to Anaktuvuk Pass that July was a beautiful flight. Andy flew through many mountain passes with snow covering the high mountains on either side. How he knew which pass to follow I found hard to fathom, but he had been flying through this area for a number of years. Even with the limited panel equipment—with just the turn and ball signals and altimeter I never saw him make a mistake. He always landed where we were supposed to land, and always with seeming ease.

As we approached the village, I could see a group of buildings in the center of a plain between the mountain peaks. Interspersed between them were white tents, difficult to see with all the snow covering everything as far as I could see. There was a freshwater lake close by the village with no ice on it. Lucky for us, since we were on floats. This was the only landing area and the lake was not very big. With a swoosh we landed. The nurse and I climbed out of the plane stepping on one of the floats to reach the snow-covered land where our smiling Eskimo greeters helped us. They had come for the mail and the supplies that Andy had brought, and to see the strange new doctor.

Very close by was an old Quonset hut. We gathered up our supplies and walked over to the Quonset hut that had been left over from World War II. Andy had the key for the door to let us in, then helped to carry all our supplies. He then disappeared to the other end of the large empty room to find the generator to get some heat started to warm us all up. We were chilled after we had walked through the snow. At the end of the empty room was a small table. On and by this we put all our medical supplies. Andy managed to find a small screen and chair to give our patients some privacy—though it was not much.

There were long benches lining the sides of the Quonset hut where our patients could sit as they came in to be examined. As I looked out of the entrance from our only door, I saw a tall, stately, beautiful woman approaching, accompanied by a number of the villagers. She had, by far and away, the most beautiful parka and boots I had ever seen. She came in slowly, holding herself erect, then stood by the bench on the left side of the room. She first placed a small blanket on the bench, and then she shook herself ever so slightly, reached back into her parka and removed a tiny baby with not a stitch on. She placed the baby carefully on the bench; she shook herself again, reached back and, lo and behold, out came another baby just a little bit older, also with no more dress than the first. She carefully placed this one by the first baby. Then, once again, she shook herself, reached back and pulled out a third small one no more than two years of age. Not one had even a semblance of a diaper on. This scene was imprinted on my mind so firmly that I have never forgotten it. Of course I checked this family unit quickly so the small ones wouldn't get cold. As I did, she replaced one after another into the back of her parka.

Something that I noted after a while was that almost every woman of childbearing age was pregnant and as far as I could determine women outnumbered the men two to one. Apparently a large number of the men had died in the measles epidemic the year before. In fact, the measles epidemic had almost wiped out the village, despite Dr. Rabeau's valiant efforts.

The next thing I found was that a number of the women had good-sized goiters, enlargements of the thyroid gland, in the front of

114

the neck. This was unusual I thought, because I had heard that they all ate many fish from the lake. Later on that day when we were visiting the trader, we were told that the lake was a freshwater lake and the fish therefore contained no iodine. Without iodine—vital to the thyroid gland— in their diets, they developed goiters. Why the men did not develop goiters I do not know.

When I talked to the white trader at dinner, we found that the salt he sold in his little store had no iodine. He readily agreed to stock iodized salt. Thus, with that question answered, no more new goiters developed in the village from that time on. I did take one woman back to Tanana with me because her goiter was so large that it caused pressure symptoms on her trachea, the breathing tube. She needed surgery. Fortunately, we were able to get her transferred from Tanana to the hospital in Mt. Edgecomb where she did have her surgery successfully.

While we were in the middle of clinic, we suddenly heard the sound of loud pounding hoofs. All of the young men in the room rushed out, grabbing their shotguns as they went. They ran to get their dogs hooked up to their sleds and off they went with their guns on their backs. Within a few minutes, we heard…bang, bang, bang. They were good shots and brought down a number of the caribou herd that had just passed us by. The villagers were in need of meat, so everyone was happy.

After the last patient had been seen, the nurse and I walked around the village. We were invited into one of the tents where we were able to check an older woman who was too sick to come to the Quonset hut. It was quite warm inside because of a small fire on the floor in the middle of the tent, protected by a metal base and a vent in the tent above for the smoke to disperse. These tents were the summer homes and were very comfortable. We examined and treated the woman, then had a cup of tea with her. A large pot was on the stove already bubbling with a caribou dinner. The women had rapidly butchered the caribou with all the villagers having a share. The men did the shooting and retrieving of the caribou and the women did the butchering. The children sat on the floor with us sucking on the bones to get the rich, fatty marrow. Raw it was, a great treat. We walked a bit more after our visit to see the solid round or square wood homes, apparently one or two rooms each, with the roofs covered by caribou skins and with the dogs tied by the side. The skins hung over the front of the homes with caribou antlers over the door.

The dogs were beautiful with thick brown or black coats mixed with white wagging tails and bright eyes, eager to go pull the sleds again. The nurse and I then joined the trader for dinner that evening along with Andy, and we had a delicious meal of fresh caribou.

The trader was a single man. I wondered how he managed, but never found out. He certainly was a good cook. The walls of his dining area were covered with shelves that were filled with canned goods of all sorts, as well as the non-iodized salt that was soon to be replaced with iodized salt.

Because we had worked so long and the dusk of midsummer night was upon us, we decided to stay the night. The Quonset was to be our home. Andy worked with the generator so we could continue to have heat during the night. We found a few oil lamps that we lit. Dinner had been great at the traders so we three bunked down in the Quonset hut. Andy had a bunch of sleeping bags in his plane for emergencies and these kept us warm. We talked late into the night, but were up early to eat some of the World War II rations that Andy found in the back of the Quonset. I liked the chocolate bar but not the peanut butter crackers. The cheese was okay but a bit stale.

After our novel breakfast, we took off in Andy's plane to head for home with our one patient with the goiter. Most all of the Eskimo villagers came out to see us off. Andy took us all the way back to Tanana. There we went right back to work in the hospital on our usual schedule.

To their credit, none of my pilots ever charged me for any time other than the hours when we were actually in the air, even when we stayed in the various villages up and down the rivers, while they waited for the clinics to be over. They held kids for me when I had to pull teeth or set a broken bone. They helped carry my gear to the schoolhouse, the trader's or wherever we held clinic.

I cannot give praise enough to those pilots. Garfield Hansen, who moved to Tanana for us, later losing his life when he crashed into the Yukon River in a white out; Andy Anderson from Bettles, who flew me all over the magnificent Brooks Range into Anaktuvuk Pass and up and down the Koyukuk River; Bob Byers from Fairbanks, who helped me rescue a crashed plane of another friend; and Mike Jones from nearby Manley Hot Springs, who carried me over the swollen river overflow in Kaltag. Not one ever turned down a call for help.

These pilots were my friends. I could never have functioned without them.

Dog team in Anaktuvuk Pass, 1954

Dog team in front of Quonset hut in Anaktuvuk Pass

Andy Anderson helping to set up clinic in the Quonset hut in Anaktuvuk

Patients coming to clinic in the Quonset hut in Anaktuvuk Pass

Carol Brandes with two little Eskimo children in Anaktuvuk Pass

Andy Anderson working on the heater to keep the Quonset hut warm

Warmly dressed Eskimo man in front of the Quonset hut and the oil drums

One of the beautiful outhouses in Wiseman, 1955

Wiseman

On one of our field trips to Anaktuvuk Pass, Andy Anderson, our pilot, suggested that we stop in the tiny village of Wiseman, sixty miles north of Bettles, also across the Arctic Circle. No doctor had stopped there in many years.

He told me that there were two factions in this village with a population of only twelve people. These two groups were not particularly friendly with one another. In fact, there was great rivalry between the two.

Andy told me of the time when there was a big fight about who would be postmaster when the old one was about to retire. There was such a commotion and name calling, and then letter writing to the postal headquarters, the Governor of Alaska and even to the President of the United States, that a group of VIPs from Washington, DC, flew out to Wiseman to meet the characters involved. The VIPs settled the dispute by making Andy the mail distributor. More of this story can be found in Andy's book, Arctic Bush Pilot.

At any rate, we stopped in Wiseman, where indeed, the people were happy to see a doctor. Unfortunately, we had to hold two clinics: one for one group and another for the other one. In addition, we had to hold them in two different places because neither group would agree to being checked anywhere near the other. All the time I was there, I heard muttering about the group that I was not checking, to which I made no comment.

The clinic was short. Nothing acute was found and the only thing that slowed us up was suturing a laceration and giving immunization shots.

The outhouses were somewhat picturesque, one having a full glass pane looking toward the magnificent mountains. It had a latch, but it was on the outside of the door!

As soon as everyone in the village had been checked, we returned to the plane and headed on north to Anaktuvuk Pass.

KALTAG

The village of Kaltag was the farthest away of my villages, about 240 miles southwest of Tanana on the Yukon River. Approximately seventy Alaska Natives, mostly Eskimos, were living there.

Beside the two white schoolteachers who lived in the apartment attached to the schoolhouse, there was a CAA family who lived on the outskirts of the village. These kind CAA people invited my nurse, my pilot Hansen, and me to have dinner and to stay with them when we were through with our clinic in the schoolhouse.

One of my summer trips to Kaltag in 1954 turned out to be an interesting and somewhat strange field clinic.

As usual, we had brought our small X-ray machine in Hansen's plane from the hospital in Tanana. With this we could take chest X-rays of all the villagers. We were trying to track down all the tuberculosis cases in my area. Having no X-ray technician, my nurse, Mary O'Tier learned to do this work on her own and was an invaluable assistant.

I examined the X-ray films taken on our return to Tanana, then they were sent on to the Public Health Department in Anchorage where the German radiologist, Dr. Karola Reitlinger, would examine them. All those with active TB would be placed on a list so we could get them either into Tanana hospital, Mt. Edgecomb, the new Anchorage ANS hospital, or into a sanatorium "Outside" in Washington state as soon a bed was available. There were never enough beds for the many TB patients, so many patients died while waiting for a bed.

Early on, we had no remedies for the patients in the villages who were waiting for a bed. One of the saddest radio calls I remember was the one I made to a man in Kaltag to let him know that a bed had finally become available for him. He refused, though he was obviously quite ill, because, "…when my son was dying with tuberculosis, coughing up blood, you had no room for him. So I will not come." He died shortly thereafter.

The only treatment we could offer the patients out in the villages with obvious symptoms of tuberculosis, was to have them lie on the affected side, use ice packs for the painful areas and give them Phenobarbital, a mild sedative, which of course was of no value in treating the tuberculosis disease.

When we reached Kaltag on that trip, the nurse and I set up our equipment in the schoolroom that the schoolteachers, a middle-aged married couple, had all ready for us. Mary O'Tier had one corner of the room to do the chest X-rays, and wearing her lead apron, she was all set to do the chest X-rays as soon as I had finished doing the exams and given the necessary treatments. To my surprise, the teachers had arranged my part of the large schoolroom with chairs in a big circle. A larger chair with a table for my equipment was placed in the center of the circle. This way, everyone seated in the chairs could observe closely what happened to each one, whom the teachers called "the victim." The teachers stood in the doorway leading to the kitchen watching my every move. They turned out to also be missionaries of some strange sect, one I had never heard about. They prayed aloud while I was checking the patients, which I must say was an unpleasant distraction.

Then, as each one approached the "victim's" chair, they would burst into a song, seemingly made up for the occasion. "Oh, you poor, poor soul, about to be tormented. May God help you in this time of your distress. May you be strong enough to bear the pain." On and on they sang. I didn't make any comment, although I certainly did want to say something to quiet them down. But, in a way, I was using their facilities, although the school was under the state government and they were state employees. Sooner or later I knew I would have to do or say something. What to do, I did not know. The Natives sat quietly in the room making no comment. I had the feeling that they were used to the teacher's "holy" songs and prayers.

In addition to all of the Natives in the schoolroom, two Army helicopter pilots who were doing some survey work in the village, joined us in the schoolroom. They were curious to see what we were doing. They also seemed to be intrigued by the teachers.

When they first came in, they offered us a ride to the CAA when we were through with the clinic. Both the nurse and I were delighted at the chance to ride in a helicopter and accepted readily. Of course the pilots had a long, long wait because we worked the whole day. But they were game and stayed. At noon the teachers were most hospitable, bringing Mary O'Tier and the two helicopter pilots, as well as me, some soup and sandwiches that we ate during a short break. After lunch we went right back to work checking each one of the patients for sore throat, skin infections, and pain in various parts of the body. Some of the exams were difficult with so many eyes watching our every move.

The most common complaint was toothache. Too much candy and coke from the traders had ruined many teeth, one of the many contributions to the Alaska Natives from the white man.

As usual, I removed the offending tooth or teeth, dropping them in a bucket so I could count them up at the end of the day to make an accurate report to the BIA about dental conditions in the bush, hoping that the information would encourage the BIA to recruit a dentist.

Just as I thought I could no longer tolerate these dreadful "hymns" a tooth with a huge cavity that I was trying to remove broke off at the roots. Looking desperately for my treasured dental elevator that the dentist in Mt Edgecomb had given me, I was at a loss. It was not to be found.

So I asked one of the teachers for a hammer. They both looked aghast, "A hammer?"

"Yes, do you have a hammer?"

They still just stood and looked at me. "A hammer, a regular claw hammer?" Both turned absolutely green, but the male teacher left the room returning with a regular hammer.

As he returned with the hammer in hand, the villagers all stood up and silently filed out of the room, remaining outside the school door until it was their turn to be called. The teachers left the room as well and did not return until the clinic was over. The pilots remained, but they did not sing. Peace—it was wonderful.

After cleaning the hammerhead with alcohol, I finished the extraction with success. Fortunately I did have anesthetic, Novocain with Ephedrine that I injected before the extraction.

Hansen stayed in the room with me, too, and was a great help. He held the kids while I checked their ears, throat, teeth and chests, then pulled whatever teeth that were causing pain.

He did this even after one of the little boys bit his finger. After that he learned to keep his fingers out of the way. Hansen, like all of the pilots I flew with to the villages helped me in so many ways. They always stood by in case I might need them.

At the end of the day I counted up the teeth in the bucket. There were 247 of them.

Before we left the school with the helicopter pilots, the teachers called me into their bedroom and plied me with sexual questions of all sorts, in particular about man and animals. I was still pretty naive but I learned a lot from these so-called religious teachers. They were bizarre. After I returned home to Tanana I turned in my report of the trip and shortly thereafter the teachers departed from Kaltag.

One of the highlights of the trip to the CAA was the short flight in the helicopter. Although we had a fishwheel in Tanana for the hospital I had never actually seen a salmon caught in one. The helicopter pilots hovered over one of the Native fishwheels and stayed until we saw one huge salmon caught by the wheel, then watched as it slid down into the waiting wood holding box. There it remained until the Native owner came for it, that is, unless a bear beat him to his catch.

We had worked so very hard and we were all tired. We had a good dinner with the CAA couple: salmon, fresh salad, veggies from their garden and brownies, my favorite, for dessert; then to bed, where we all slept the sleep of the dead. In the morning, after finishing up with a few more patients at the school, this time traveling via the CAA man's boat, we headed back to Tanana.

ANCHORAGE

Prior to leaving Tanana, a young man by the name of Bernardus Smit (Ben), from Fairbanks, was sent to our village to supervise the rebuilding of our Northern Commercial Company (NC) store that had burned to the ground, at a time when Ronnie Humphries had been the manager. Ben was a trouble-shooter for the NC Company and had been sent out to Tanana to oversee this rather large construction project. He had to stay for a fairly long period that summer in 1955 and he frequently came to our hospital parties and dances.

Ben told me that he had been working on his PhD when he left Leidin University in Holland, to come to live in the USA. He also told me that he spoke eight languages, including Malaysian. At first I did not like him at all, but he was very bright, tall, and extremely charming. As the summer of 1955 continued on, he finally wore down my defenses and I agreed to marry him. My father, who had been visiting in Tanana, met him, and was vocally upset with my decision and stopped writing his weekly letter to me for over two years.

However, we were married by Bishop Gordon in Tanana, in June of 1956. My brother Stan who was in seminary school flew up from Sewanee, Tennessee, to give me away.

Ben had received a transfer from the Fairbanks NC store to the NC base store in Anchorage. There was no problem for me to get a transfer to the ANS hospital in Anchorage since the hospital there was still very short of doctors.

On arriving in Anchorage, I found that I made the eighth staff general practice doctor, with the MOC, a specialist in internal medicine. This was a hospital with four hundred inpatient beds, one half of which were for tuberculosis patients and a very active outpatient clinic. We all, except for the MOC, shared night call and the clinic duties. We were busy.

My duties included being the liaison between the hospital and the town doctors. These included Doctors William Mills (orthopedics), Helen Whaley and John Tower (pediatricians), Milo Fritz, Joe Shelton, and Wally Dunn (EENT), and Bob Whaley (internist), who consulted with the ANS staff. We also had a dentist, Doctor Jerry Morrow, who fulfilled a much-needed part of the hospital work.

The pediatric wards were mine. Ninety beds in all, forty-five were filled with tuberculosis children, the other forty-five had a mixture of pneumonias, abdominal disorders, cardiac patients, seizure patients and a variety of other diseases.

Each day I made rounds, one day with Helen Whaley, the other with John Tower, learning a lot from each. When anyone of my patients went to surgery or to have some other procedure done, I was first assistant.

We were busy all the time. When we were on call, we delivered babies, took care of acute problems on any of the wards, and saw emergency outpatients in the clinic. Finally, we got a surgeon, Doctor Moles, who drove a Jaguar, which impressed us all. We were lucky my second year, in 1957, to get another good general practitioner, Doctor Gloria Park, who remained with the ANS hospital longer than any of the other doctors until she retired in 1985.

Ben and I lived first in a duplex on 20th Street by Lake Otis Parkway, near Gloria Park, then bought a house on F Street, right downtown for our second year. At this time, there were only one and a half paved streets in town and there was only one major hotel, the Westward Hotel, now called the Hilton Hotel. The Fourth Avenue theater and the Empress theater were the only movie houses. And when downtown Providence Hospital decided to move out to its present location on Providence Drive in the early '60s, everyone laughed, saying that no one would ever go there because it would be so far out of town!

Time passed quickly. Ben was often out of town, visiting Northern Commercial stores around Alaska. I never knew when he would be coming home, so my social life was limited.

After two years in Anchorage, Ben received a promotion. He was transferred from Anchorage to the Bethel NC store as manager.Our story of this move to western Alaska will be covered in a later chapter in this book.

Four hundred-bed ANS hospital in Anchorage, 1956

Another view of Anchorage ANS hospital, 1956

THE PRIBILOF ISLAND OF ST. PAUL

Shortly after I transferred from Tanana to the ANS hospital in Anchorage, the Medical Officer in Charge announced at our weekly staff meeting that the doctor at St. Paul, the larger of the two Pribilof Islands, was ill. The Pribilofs are about 600 miles west of Anchorage, 310 of these miles across the Bering Sea. Someone was needed to replace him for two weeks. I quickly volunteered to go before someone else did. I had wanted to go to the Pribilofs because I always wanted to go where I had never been before and the Pribilofs sounded like an exciting place to go. Immediately I was accepted as the temporary replacement.

In the morning, after hastily packing, I was on the weekly plane to St. Paul. I took my jeans, two sweaters, some warm mitts and two white doctor jackets along with a few other necessities. The bouncy five-hour flight in a DC 3 ended with a smooth landing on St. Paul's long and paved landing strip.

When I landed on the field at St. Paul, I found the island windswept and almost deserted. Fortunately, the weather was good, slightly overcast, but not raining. The temperature was in the low forties, but the biting wind made me happy to have my warm parka. I soon found that the wind was always present. Sometimes it blew more, sometimes less, an unforgiving wind.

When we landed on the airfield at St. Paul, very few people were in sight, There had been no other passengers on the plane, just a lot of freight to be unloaded; food supplies for the grocery store, equipment for all sorts of uses, building supplies, repair materials for the electrical system, and more boxes that had oddball markings that I couldn't figure out. The one person I saw standing by was the chief officer of Fish and Wildlife, the man who ran the island in many ways. He was there to meet me. He was tall and slender, all wrapped up in what was obviously an old well-worn parka. He greeted me warmly and voiced his concern about the doctor who did not seem to be improving.

"Doctor Persons, we are putting you up in the hotel rather than the doctor's house. Each morning the cooks will come to prepare your meals. We have an excellent nurse who will show you around and help you in any way she can. She has been caring for the doctor, as well as the clinic patients until you arrived. If there is anything you need, just let me know."

He was so friendly that I felt right at home, excited to be on St. Paul. We walked to the one and only hotel, he carrying my bag as he told me a little about St. Paul. The hotel loomed up in front of us after a brief fifteen-minute walk. It was a huge, old three-story frame building, the outer boards brown and weathered. There was a long reception desk in front of us as we walked in the unlocked door, but no receptionist was in sight. The building squeaked and squealed as the wind howled through the cracks between the boards. After a while I would become used to the ever-present wind. It served to remind me to wear my parka every time I ventured outside.

He guided me to the right down a long dark hallway to the room that was to be mine. The dentist normally occupied the next room but he was away on vacation. My room was large and airy with a king size bed with a bedside table on which was a single lamp; a dresser, a large closet and a sink with running hot and cold water.

The two windows in my room opened directly onto the unpaved gravel road by the hotel. The bathroom was all the way down at the end of that dark hallway. The windows were so low that on opening them, one could step in or out of the room onto the gravel road. There was no lock or latch on my door, nor was there any on the front door of the hotel. Anyone could wander in and out of the hotel at any time, a fact that was a bit scary.

I had the whole hotel all to myself. This would change once the tourist season began in June, two and a half months from my arrival time. In the meantime the hotel was mine alone. I was a bit uneasy with this arrangement because of the lack of security.

My guide told me that in the morning the cooks would come to make my breakfast at seven thirty. So they did, both young men, making me a splendid breakfast each and every morning in the huge old kitchen. In the early mornings, I could hear them starting the old gas stove. This noise served as my alarm clock. They cooked me breakfast every morning, but there was always way too much food, so much that I could never eat it all. Scrambled eggs, bacon, sausage, pancakes, hot cereal, even waffles if I wished. The cooks were obliging and seemed to enjoy their work, though they rarely spoke to me. They smiled in answer to my questions, and I was not sure if they understood me. There was no way that I could eat all of my breakfast, but I am sure they were happy to have all the leftovers. Maybe that was part of the reason for the very generous servings.

The next morning I was taken to the ailing doctor's quarters. It was a well-built two-story whitewashed frame house, large enough for a family of five or six. The occupant was a very young doctor, in his late twenties, obviously grateful for my coming to relieve him. He was quite ill, running an extremely high fever and a severe sore throat. Within fifteen minutes, I was able to clinically diagnose his illness as infectious mononucleosis, later to be confirmed by laboratory tests. He needed fluids and a good bit of medical care. He also wanted someone to clean his house, cook for him and keep him entertained.

Taking care of his medical problems I was happy to do, but not the rest. It wasn't easy for him to turn his medical work over to me. He was worried that I might not be able to give good care to the Natives to whom he was devoted. Finally, since he was quite ill, he had to capitulate in letting me take over. A few days later, I got on the evening radio call to give the Anchorage MOC my assessment of the situation on St.Paul. I told my Anchorage chief that I had the medical work well under control but that the young doctor needed to be transferred to Anchorage. He was just too much for me. Thus he was sent out on the next plane to Anchorage, where he was hospitalized.

Before the doctor left, he gave me his pistol saying, "Here Jean, you will need this for protection, sooner or later." I did take it, though at the time it was only to keep peace with him.

The engineer who escorted me on my daily afternoon walks told me a bit about St. Paul as we walked. The temperature was only in the low forties, but the wind was chilling and without our parkas, mitts, and boots we would have been frozen.

The icy water lapping on the rocky volcanic beaches, the howling wind, the noise from all of the birds as they flew above us, chirping and squawking, and the terrible isolation made St. Paul a place of total fascination to me. The engineer told me that over 750,000 seals would return from their journey down south as far as California in early April. One old bull remained on the island to guide the others back with his loud roaring that could be heard all over the island. The seals came back to the island each spring to breed, the bulls fighting over the females as they established their territory with their harems. Once the baby seals were born, the mothers nursed them for the summer before the babies ventured into the water to hunt fish for themselves. Three million birds also returned for the same purpose, to breed. Sandhill cranes, kittiwakes, auklets, murres, as well as my favorites, the puffins. Ducks and geese joined the throng.

Although I had looked forward to seeing the thousands of seals as they arrived from the south, I dreaded the harvest by clubbing that would follow, with the skinning process for the skins, which would then be sold. These supplied the major source of income on the island. Fortunately for me, the seals did not return before my departure. I could not have faced the slaughter.

The engineer told me a little about the Aleuts. They had been so named by the Russians, although they called themselves Unangan meaning "The People" and had their own language. They were racially similar to the Siberian people and to the Eskimos in western Alaska. They were great hunters, using their skin kayaks to hunt sea otters and to fish. Originally they had come from Atka Island on the Aleutian chain, but before this from eastern Asia. When the Russians came for the sea otters and sealskins, they brought many infectious diseases including tuberculosis, which caused a large number of the Aleuts to die.

There were no trees on St. Paul. The black rocks and dark grainy sand on the beaches that resulted from old volcanic activity added to the barren appearance of the island.

Housing for everyone was supposedly excellent, though the frame buildings the government had built for the Natives were not totally wind-proof, and cracks in the walls let in some of the persistent wind. Many of the houses had basements outfitted with photography developing equipment. Of course, the Fish and Wildlife personnel had the very best of all the homes.

There was one church on the island, the Russian Orthodox, with a kind, but firm older priest who had been there for a number of years. Though the Natives disliked the Russians because of their cruel treatment, they liked the Russian priests. The priests gave the people respect both for their culture and their language.

The Russian priest often invited me to dinner, which was always excellent, both the food and the company. I felt it was a great honor to be invited. He had so many tales to tell of the people and of his work with them. It was easy to see by how the Natives spoke of him, that he was much beloved by his congregation.

It was an experience to go the church services. I had never been to a Russian Orthodox church before. The men sat on one side of the church, the women on the other. Once the service started everyone stood for the whole time, and the services lasted for a long time, about three hours. I always went up to the balcony, because from there I had an excellent view of the church and all the people, plus, I could lean against the balcony rail.

The priest warned me about what would happen after Easter was over. He told me that a lot of the young men would be drinking. No one touched alcohol during Lent because of the instructions given by the priest, so the young men would get rather wild when Lent was over. There would be a great deal of singing, dancing and lots of drinking. Then there was no telling what else might happen. He did note that nine months after Easter there would be an unusual number of babies born.

I went to bed about ten o'clock on Easter evening with the doctor's pistol under my pillow, though generally I kept it on the bedside table, then went right to sleep. About three in the morning, I was awakened by footsteps going back and forth on the dirt road outside my windows. Back and forth, back and forth, getting closer and closer all the time. I had opened one of the windows about six inches, because I liked fresh air at night, despite the wind. All one had to do was to push the window up a bit to be able to step right into my room. I was scared.

When the steps became very close to my window I figured I'd better say something. I called out "Who is there?" hoping that my voice was not too quivery.

"Doctor, I have heart trouble."

"Tell me, what symptoms are you having?"

"My head hurts," he replied. His voice was slightly slurred.

"Do you have pain any where else or any other problems?"

"No, I just feel bad."

"Tell me more. How old are you?"

"Twenty five," he replied.

"Are you short of breath?"

"No, but I don't feel so good."

"I think your trouble is that you have had too much to drink. Come to the clinic first thing in the morning and I'll examine you then."

After a few more questions, I decided his problem was not his heart, at least not a medical heart problem. He sounded pretty drunk and none of his symptoms rang true. I told him that I did not think he had any problem with his heart and that if he came into my room I would shoot him. I also told him that the doctor, when he had given me the pistol, had told me to shoot anyone who bothered me in the leg. I told the young man this, but told him that I was not going to shoot him in the leg, because then I would be up the rest of the night patching him up. Therefore, if he did come in through my window, I was going to shoot him through his heart. Of course, my hand holding the pistol was shaking so hard, I probably could not have hit the side of a barn. I told him that I wanted him to come to the clinic at ten o'clock in the morning so I could check him out properly.

Fortunately for me, the young man took my words seriously. "Okay, Doctor, I'll come in the morning." Slowly, very slowly, the footsteps faded away. Finally, I put the pistol down on my bedside table. But there was no sleeping for me the rest of the night. I kept listening to be sure he did not change his mind.

In the morning, in the middle of clinic, someone called me. There was a young man outside who looked about thirty years of age. With a sheepish smile on his face, and no doubt, a terrible hangover, he said, "Doctor, I've come to apologize for last night. I didn't mean to scare you." He was so nice I accepted his apology, but told him if he did have any problems I would be more than happy to check him out.

Once he left, the story of his nocturnal visit spread over the island, and I had all sorts of offers to help if I had any further difficulties. The best offer came from the engineer. He came and fixed my windows with nails so they could not be opened more than six inches. He also put a latch on my door so no one could just walk in. This would have been easy with the hotel unlocked, and no receptionist. Just me alone in that big old hotel with all its creaking and wheezing with the winds that never ceased.

My final week on the island brought the dentist back from his vacation. He had the room next to me. He sang at the top of his voice all the time, when he was not asleep or at work. It did not bother me one least little bit. I was so happy to have someone else in the building with me. Before I left he made me a pair of earrings out of some shells and denture material. I kept them for years.

The clinic was small, with benches outside of the exam room for the patients to sit on. Save for emergencies I saw each person in turn, just as I had done in Tanana. I did note, as I called a patient in one morning, that the wife of one of the higher-ranking Fish and Wildlife men was there. She started to get up when I called the next patient. I told her it was not her turn quite yet, but I would see her as soon as her turn came. She was obviously angry and stalked out.

She and her husband had invited me to dinner that night. One of the first things she said to me as we sat down at the table, "I guess you didn't realize who I was this morning at the clinic."

"Oh yes," I told her, "but I've always had a policy that each patient should be seen in turn." That was only fair. I then went on to tell her that in Tanana I had always followed this rule and that it had worked out well. Even if the patient was an animal, dog, wounded lynx, or other wild animal that was brought in, each patient, human or otherwise was still taken in turn. Somehow she didn't seem impressed, just complained about her headache that she had had that morning. I was not invited back.

The clinic was not well equipped. There were no disposable needles and the old needles we had to use had actual barbs on the tips. I was lucky enough to have a most efficient nurse to help me. She had been on St. Paul for years. She and I would sit in the late afternoons sharpening the needles on a special stone. Then we sterilized them in alcohol. Not a very satisfactory use of time, but the patients seemed to appreciate our efforts.

The week the young doctor was due to return, we had a big snowstorm, so his flight was cancelled. It gave me one more week on the island and I was not sorry.

One of the first things I did when I returned to Anchorage was to be sure my order for syringes with disposable needles was filled and shipped out to St. Paul.

For several years, I had frequent long letters from the doctor on St. Paul. A good physician, but a very lonesome man.

The Russian Orthodox priest in front of his church on St. Paul, one of the two Pribilof islands

Housing for the top government officials on St. Paul

Jean resting after a long cold walk around the island of St. Paul, 1956

Seals on the island of St. Paul

Dark baby seal on St. Paul

Light-colored baby seal on St. Paul

EARLY BETHEL

In May of 1958, Ben (my former husband), was offered a job as manager of the Bethel Northern Commercial Company (NC) that included the NC store, the movie house, the cold storage and the Exxon gas station. It was an opportunity too good to turn down. Ben had been a trouble-shooter for the NC Company and had stayed in Tanana while the Tanana NC store was being rebuilt following the fire that destroyed the store.

Going to Bethel had not been in my plans, but it was easy to get transferred from the Anchorage ANS hospital where I had served for two years after coming down from Tanana, to the ANS hospital in Bethel without difficulty—the Bethel hospital had only two doctors at that time. So, we packed up, sold our home on F Street in Anchorage and headed west to Bethel, where we would live in NC housing across the road from the store for the next four years.

Bethel at that time had a population of twelve hundred, mixed Alaska Natives and whites, the majority of the inhabitants being Eskimo. Bethel was built on the banks of the Kuskokwim River. It is located in the southwest part of Alaska, about three hundred miles west from Anchorage.

The ANS hospital territory included nineteen widely scattered villages, not one connected to another by road. Most all of the village sites were to be found either on the banks of the Kuskokwim River or alongside various smaller tributary rivers that ran into the main Kuskokwim River.

I wanted to take my VW Beetle that I had had bought in Fairbanks for $600 dollars after I married Ben and before leaving Tanana. At first, the Beetle would not fit into the DC3. After much trying, the airplane crew took off the left side of the car. Then it fit into the airplane without difficulty.

It was a six-hour flight from Anchorage to Bethel, with a stopover in McGrath where we had decided to spend the night. McGrath was a very tiny village, having only a handful of people living there. The roadhouse was owned, as I remember, by two old men. It had a bar on the main floor with a good supple of alcohol. Our room was on the second floor. The roadhouse was a rather rickety frame building and there was always fear of fire. There were no fire engines in any of the villages. If fire occurred there would be only a bucket brigade. In our room, for safety, we had a coiled rope ladder lying by the window.. Fortunately we didn't need it.

The next morning, after a large breakfast of bacon and eggs, we took off for Bethel. When we landed in Bethel we found that the airfield was on an island across the Kuskokwim River from Bethel. Some of the crew helped put the VW back together. Ben had already arranged for one of the NC barges to come over to pick us up after the aircraft landed.

It was quite a scary trip because the river ran rapidly and not smoothly. To get the car on the barge we had to drive it over two planks of wood laid down, one end on the land and the other on the barge. The planks were bouncy and everyone stood around to watch. Then when we reached the other side of the river, the same procedure was followed in reverse also with a group of onlookers. I added several white hairs to my head on this trip, but we did survive.

On our arrival, the VW made the sixth car in Bethel. When we left Bethel four years later we sold the Beetle to pilot Ray Christiansen for $800. Cars were in great demand.

The new hospital had seventy-five beds. There was the MOC, Dr. Brownlee, a surgeon. John Schulz and I were the two general practitioners. When I walked into Dr. Brownlee's office I reached out my hand to greet the MOC. Instead, he looked at me and said, "Jean, are you saved?"

I had never heard this phrase before and quickly looked over my shoulder half expecting to see a bear or some other wild thing or who knows what. Shortly afterward I learned that he was very religious and the question referred to his religious group. I had no idea how to respond to my new boss.

John Shultz was an exceptional doctor and we became good friends. He and his wife lived in hospital quarters across the road from the hospital. The living quarters supplied for the doctors were quite luxurious for Bethel, having two or three bedrooms and indoor plumbing with hot and cold running water. These were extremely convenient for times when we were on call, particularly in the wee hours. However,

138

because of Ben's work, I stayed downtown in the NC quarters driving the VW Beetle to the hospital daily and whenever I was on call.

The hospital was much larger than my thirty-bed hospital in Tanana but we had a fine staff of nurses and nurses aides, who were mostly Eskimo, plenty of maintenance crew, a hospital manager and a well-staffed kitchen crew.

At this point there was a big push to get the doctors to sign up in the Public Health Service. Way back, in 1902, there was a conversion of the Marine Hospital Service to Public Health and Marine Service. In 1912 this name was shortened to the Public Health Service. The Public Health Service took over from the BIA in 1956 and the first thing that happened was that a ton more paper work was piled onto the doctors, and the doctors in the Service were supposed to wear uniforms for all official holidays.

If one did join, the Public Health Service could transfer the doctors to other Public Health facilities in Alaska or to one of the Indian reservations Outside. I preferred to keep my freedom, so remained a civilian doctor for all my time in Alaska. Only one other doctor in Alaska did the same while working for the ANS hospital in Anchorage, Dr. Gloria Park. The rest chose to join the Public Health Service.

The Bethel hospital had a huge waiting room. The receptionists stood behind a long desk with all the charts in the cabinets behind them. The receptionists were experienced in sorting the patients, the acutely ill, those who were wounded or bleeding, the pregnant ones near term and so on.

We had no medical students to help us, and the only visiting doctors who came out for special clinics that I can recall were the pediatrician, Dr Helen Whaley, and the orthopedic doctor, Dr. William Mills, who came for a number of clinics.

One doctor was on duty in the clinic area, which filled rapidly in the morning—patients coming not only from Bethel, but also from all the other villages that were included in the hospital area. We had two exam rooms separated by a curtain. Each had a small dressing room. Many of the patients spoke only a few words of English so I had an Eskimo interpreter who was a medical assistant. We kept our medications on a couple of shelves so we could dispense them as necessary.

We had no pharmacy and there was none in the town. Elsie was my assistant for the years that I was doing my time in the clinic. She was a remarkable young woman who could have become an excellent physician, had she had the chance.

We three permanently-assigned doctors rotated the clinic and ward work, doing radio call to the villages in the evening, taking call every third night and every third weekend. Here, as in Tanana, no one gave any thought to overtime pay.

The three of us mostly put in eight to twelve-hour days because there were so many patients. If they were there, they were seen. If there were emergencies we all worked together. The doctor in the clinic sent the acutely ill or the women in active labor, straight to the wards. One time, I had a patient who gave me no time to have her taken to the delivery room, so I delivered her on the exam table in the clinic, a few minutes after she had climbed up on the table for her prenatal check-up.

Our radio room was just big enough for a table to hold the radio, a space to write the messages, and room enough for a chair. Just as in Tanana, many of the villagers in the area listened in to all the questions and advice given. At times we had to send a pilot out to pick up an emergency.

Down the hall of the hospital were two wards: one for OB (obstetrics) and the other a general ward for fractures, pneumonia, liver disease, bleeding stomach ulcers, and everything else that came in. Infectious diseases were screened off at one end of the general ward. We had a surgery room that the MOC kept under his charge with either John or me as assistant during any major surgical procedure. If any one was beyond our capabilities, we could send the very complicated ones to the main ANS hospital in Anchorage.

No one was doing any fieldwork in the surrounding villages, but after a bit of pushing, the MOC agreed to start field trips. As in my previous work in Tanana, many of the Alaska Natives could not manage to get into Bethel except on occasion. No roads existed between the villages, so trips were made by small plane, if one was available, or in the summer by boat and by dog sled in the winter.

About this time I discovered that I was pregnant. Since I would be out of commission after delivery for a while, it was decided that I

140

should do all the field trips, then the other two doctors could do the trips after my baby was born.

Consequently, I did all the trips. At first all the nurses vied with one another to go with me, but as my pregnancy progressed, I noticed that the nurses, instead of wanting to go with me, were drawing straws to see who would have to go with me. Then I learned that not one of them wanted to deliver me should I go into early labor. Actually, I did go into labor on my last trip out, but then the labor stopped and I went to sleep. The nurse did not.

On these trips the nurse would check the patients who were taking tuberculosis medications. Experiments were still being run with half the population of the village taking Isoniazid, the other half a placebo. This way we could determine if the INH, as the Isoniazid was called, would help the Natives from developing active tuberculosis. The experiment was overseen by the Public Health Department in Washington DC, but we did all the groundwork as we had done in Tanana where the experiments were first run.

I would do the usual exams, treatment and dental extractions, but always I would ask my patient if he or she were really taking the pills. A number of the pregnant women would say "No, doctor, I'm pregnant and I don't want anything to hurt my baby."

Then I would say, while rubbing my stomach, "I'm pregnant and I'm taking the pills too."

"Okay, doctor, if you take them, I will too."

The reason that I was taking the tuberculosis drugs was because a young man in his early twenties had come to the hospital clinic one day when I was on duty. He began to cough up blood and then dropped dead at the front door. I rushed over to him and gave him mouth-to-mouth resuscitation, to no avail. The next day, I was on autopsy detail and had to do his autopsy. When I opened up his chest I found two huge tuberculous cavities. Since I was pregnant, and even if I hadn't been, I started myself on INH, which I took for six months. Fortunately, no problems developed.

The Public Health officials never knew that if my daughter, Michele, had not survived, that whole experimental INH study might well have been a failure.

Bethel was cold and windy in the winter, the temperature often reaching thirty degrees below zero. That was without any wind factor tied in. The wind blew across the flat tundra for hundreds of miles without any natural windbreaker. The snow in winter flew horizontally.

Living in the village was much more convenient for Ben, my then-husband to have easy access to the NC store, which was right across the unpaved road from our house. We lived in a frame building, one in a row of green company houses, all on high stilts in the event of a flood, connected to each other by a boardwalk. We heated water on the kitchen stove that we fed with coal. We washed clothes in an old-fashion washing machine that we had to churn, then put the clothes through a wringer. We hung them outside where they would freeze in winter, doing the final drying on a line over the stove. Many were the injuries that we had with kids who got their arms caught in the wringers.

In the center of our large, drafty living room we had a coal stove. It gave out plenty of heat but had a habit of going out now and then.

We had a small room for the toilet where we kept a honey bucket, using Pine Sol to cover the odors that emanated. No matter how clean we kept the room, the odor of Pine Sol is embedded in my memory.

We paid two young Native boys to collect the honey bucket three times a week. They carried it out the front door, sometimes tripping and spilling the contents on the boardwalk outside the entrance. In the summer it was easy to clean, but in winter the contents froze rapidly, causing real problems because it was not so simple to clean.

In town there were two "honey bucket" lakes, one right behind the house. These lakes received almost all the honey bucket contents in Bethel. In the winter, the lakes froze, of course, but everyone still ice-skated on them. Ben would join the groups, but I would not.

We did have a separate garage where we kept our VW Beetle. In the winter it was not easy to start, so Ben had a habit of putting a little heater under the engine to warm it up. Several times he almost burned down the whole garage when the car caught fire, but he did manage to put the fire out each time.

In Bethel, although there were a few telephone poles, most of the phone connections were on a rabbit line. The lines were just laid down over the tundra and each of us was on a party line.

My ring was two longs, one short, followed by one long. Our phone was on a table next to my side of the bed. When I was on call every third night I would wake up with each call to check if it were my call from the hospital. Mostly the calls were between the girls in town and their boy friends at the military base just out of town, If not, someone was calling the one cab we had in town. The voices were loud and clear and some of the conversations were explicit.

Unfortunately, everyone on the rabbit line heard all the calls that came through, some of which would have been very entertaining had I not needed to sleep.

Marsh's roadhouse was at the corner, across from the NC store. The only flush toilet in Bethel was in the roadhouse, so both guests and locals frequented it.

We had an outbreak of typhoid fever one year and were having a difficult time tracing the origin of the disease. We looked everywhere in town. Finally, we found the cause. The highly-prized roadhouse toilet had pipes that ran over the kitchen stove. A leak had sprung in the pipes and the drips went right down into the soup and other things cooking on the stove. Grim!

Fixing the leaks and changing the pipe location ended our search. Everyone in the village had typhoid vaccinations and the Bethel epidemic was over, except for the infected few who carried the disease out into the neighboring villages. A mass vaccination was then carried out to end the epidemic.

Ben promised me that once the baby was born he would get running water in the house. He did manage to do this by putting a large tank on top of the house. Kuskokwim River water was pumped into the tank. Life was much easier thereafter.

One important thing that Ben did was to put up a gas pump right on the banks of the Kuskokwim River between the NC store and our row of elevated NC houses. This was a great convenience for the few people who had cars and for the cab driver, saving a visit all the way out to the gas and oil depot. It also served the small float planes that landed on the river in the summer and those that landed on the frozen river in the winter. They could come close enough to the gas pump to fill up their tanks.

143

One winter day, a pilot on skis, filled the tanks of his single engine Cessna with gasoline. He then went down on the frozen river to start his engine. First he turned on the fuel switch and primed the engine. Then he got out to hand crank the propeller, pulling the propeller through five or six times. When he tried to get back into the plane he was unable to get back in time and the plane took off without him.

Unfortunately, the pilot had forgotten his very first duty, that is, to block the skis properly. His plane few up in the air, circled three times, then down the plane came, crashing a half dozen feet from the newly installed gas pump. A few feet closer and there would have been a tremendous explosion.

Life in Bethel was always interesting.

Bethel from the air, 1961

Taking a ride in my old VW Beetle in Bethel, on the Kuskokwim River,
at Christmastime looking for a Christmas tree, 1958

The Northern Commercial store in Bethel, 1958

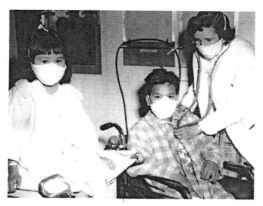

Jean with her tuberculosis patients, 1961

Northern Commercial housing with our VW Beetle stuck in the snow

Always a cold wind in Bethel

BETHEL AND MICHELE

Time passed and my delivery time was getting closer. Ben had a Northern Commercial (NC) meeting in Anchorage in the latter part of January 1959. We decided it would be better for me to stay up in the government quarters across from the hospital while he was gone. Shoveling snow at this stage of my pregnancy to get the car out of the garage, was probably not the best idea. Therefore, though it was six weeks before my due date, I moved up to the hospital area where there was a nice warm place to stay as well as an indoor shower and bath. This was true luxury.

January was a cold, snowy, and windy time, so being able to take a hot shower in my new quarters before bed was heaven. Also when I was on call, I didn't have to dig the snow away from the garage door to get the car before driving to the hospital every morning or each time I got an emergency hospital call at night.

On January 27th, my second night in my comfortable quarters, I was on call. After doing a late radio schedule with a number of villages, I made rounds on the general ward to be sure all the patients were doing okay. It was after 10 p.m. before I headed across the road to my temporary home and a nice hot shower. Then into bed. Suddenly, I realized I was in labor. Waiting a half hour to be sure, I dressed and headed back to the hospital and to the OB ward where the nurse was sitting quietly behind her desk reading a magazine, since there were no patients in labor on the floor. The nurse smiled at me. "What are you doing over here at this late hour, Doctor? We have no one on this ward."

"I've come to admit myself. I think I'm going to have my baby."

She laughed, thinking I was joking, "You've got six weeks to go. It's too early." I laughed back. She laughed and we began telling jokes, both of us having a fun time. But she suddenly became aware of the fact that some of my laughter sounded a bit painful. "You are in labor,' she finally said.

"That's why I came," I replied as I bent over, holding my stomach in pain. Quickly she took me down to get undressed and put me into bed. Then she called my friend John Schultz, who was on duty, to come check me. He found me to be in early labor. I wanted to deliver before eight in the morning before the MOC came on duty. But that was not to be.

As a first-time mother, my labor was not a quick one— 8 a.m. came and went. The MOC came into my room and just took over. Fortunately, John stayed with me in the delivery room.

Although the baby was six weeks premature, forceps were used, and as I best remember, were not released for twenty minutes. Michele was born with no heartbeat and no respirations. John did artificial respirations with mouth-to-mouth breathing and a bit of adrenaline. She was blue and totally non-responsive, but with his efforts he was able to resuscitate her. She was placed in an incubator, weighing in at five pounds, five ounces. Unfortunately, she stopped breathing frequently. The nurse would flick her feet with her thumb and that would start her breathing again. Michele had red curly hair and all the staff was in the hall waiting when we were wheeled out of the delivery room. They cheered when they saw her.

In the meantime, Ben was notified via the radio to the Anchorage Native Hospital, followed by a phone call by Dr. Rabeau to his Northern Commercial meeting, telling him that he had a daughter. He took the next flight back to Bethel.

One problem we had in the hospital was the heating arrangement. In order to keep the OB ward at seventy degrees, the general floor, that was full of a variety of patients, was over-heated with temperatures of eighty-five to ninety degrees. With this difficult problem, it was decided that I should be discharged to go back home the day after delivery, this time downtown since Ben was back. We wrapped Michele up in blankets and drove home. Ben got me settled in bed, with Michele in a well-padded cardboard box right by my bed. This way I could keep a close eye on her. I had to flick her feet almost constantly to remind her to breathe. Ben was cheerful and seemed to be happy to have a daughter.

As soon as we were settled in, Ben left to go to the NC store because he said he had a lot of catch-up work to do.

Within fifteen minutes of his departure, the coal stove in the living room blew up. Black soot and smoke was all over the house. Quickly, I covered Michele's face and took her into the bathroom, shutting the door so the soot wouldn't get in there. I grabbed my parka, boots and

148

mitts, then grabbed Michele, tucking her inside my parka. I went out in the dark, the snow was blowing and the temperature was about zero. With a flashlight I headed over the boardwalk and across the road to the NC store to find Ben. It was about 7 p.m. and there was no one there. So, off I went to find someone to help me locate him.

First off, I found an older Eskimo couple walking on the road, but they spoke no English. No help there. Finally I found one of the NC boys. When he heard my story, he promised to find Ben and send him home. I went back to the house and went into the bathroom, which had no soot in the air. I piled pillows into the non-functioning bathtub, and with a blanket to cover us, climbed into the tub with my little preemie. There we remained until Ben got home to fix the stove.

Apparently he had gone up to Ding's, the nickname of the head of the National Guard unit for Bethel and the surrounding villages. He was a single young man, who loved to have parties with the nurses from the hospital. Here Ben had gone to celebrate the birth of his daughter. The NC messenger had no problem locating him.

After this and after the air in the house had cleared, Michele and I retired to the bedroom, she again in her cardboard box by my side. She was way too small to put in her crib and with her breathing difficulty I wanted to have her right with me. She was very weak, (as was I, having lost half my blood during that grim delivery). It took her an hour to nurse, an hour to sleep, then to nurse again, with me flicking her feet each time she stopped breathing. She kept up this schedule for two weeks, then at eight pounds she was fine, I was too, after taking iron with each meal and finally getting a little sleep.

Michele was named after one of my favorite little patients in Tanana, whom I almost adopted, but didn't since at the time I was single.

After a number of weeks I went back to work at the hospital, working afternoons in the clinic. Officially, I worked four hours, but actually five hours, to be sure all the patients waiting were seen.

In the mornings when I was home, I would do the laundry, with our old fashioned washing machine. Then I would put the clothes through the hand wringer. On the left side of the house we had a clothesline. The clothes would freeze almost as soon as they were hung, but in a few hours I would bring them in to hang on the line in the kitchen over the oil stove. This worked well. No disposable diapers were available back then and Michele had a lot of diapers.

On returning home about 5 p.m., I would feed Michele right away because she was so hungry. She refused to take a bottle from my wonderful Eskimo baby sitter. Cooking dinner and cleaning up made for a full day.

Ben had promised an indoor toilet when the baby was born. He quickly hired someone to put up a huge tank on top of the roof, which held a hundred gallons of water. Our roof must have been very strong. Once a week one enterprising man in town brought water in his truck. This would be pumped up into our tank. If I remember correctly, water that came from the Kuskokwim River was forty cents a gallon. No one was to drink this water until it had been boiled on the stove for at least fifteen minutes. The reason for this was that the villages upriver dumped their garbage, dead dogs and other contaminated debris into the river. Once a dead man floated by.

As soon as Michele was strong enough, I bathed her in the now-functioning bathtub. Typical of all children, she sucked on the washrag. She had diarrhea for three weeks, then was healthy as a horse. She seemed to be immune to everything.

When Michele started to crawl, she had no ill effects, despite the floors being so cold—an ice cube on the floor would not melt. Remember the house was on stilts to protect the house from floods. As far as I could determine there was no insulation under the floor. Michele soon found where Tinker's dog food was in a bowl in the kitchen and at times she and Tinker shared the food together.

When she was three weeks old, sometime in February, we took her out on the frozen river for a picnic. Ben put two poles down into the snow, stringing a blanket between them to keep the wind away. We made a small fire, cooked our hot dogs, ate as fast as we could and went back home. Michele did well. She did not share the hot dogs.

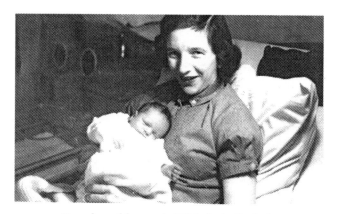

*Two-day-old premie Michele in Bethel,
just after Alaska became a state in 1959*

Michele coming out of our house which was on high stilts, Bethel, 1961

Michele getting a ride in her box with her mom, 1960

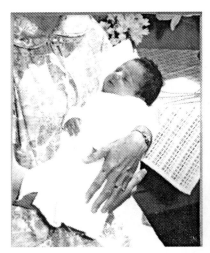

Baby Renee with lots of hair, 1960

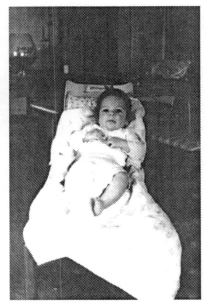

*Renee with Dr. Mills' cast
on her leg, 1960*

BETHEL AND RENEE

Before Michele was a year old, I decided that she should have a sibling. She was so cute and smart that I was afraid that we would spoil her. Within a few months I was pregnant again, but I continued to work in the clinic in the afternoons. Unfortunately, the other two doctors felt there was too much work at the hospital, so no more field trips from the Bethel hospital were done.

Three months before Renee was due, she decided to come early. Not to have the same problems I had had with Michele, I got on the first plane available to Anchorage. Here I stayed with a variety of friends, trying not to overstay my time in any one place. I didn't want to wear out my welcome with any of them.

The last place I stayed was with my nurse, Edna Borovitch. Getting closer to my delivery date, I often would have a few contractions before going to sleep. Edna would be on the alert. I would then go to sleep, she did not. On the day before Thanksgiving in 1960, my contractions began to increase. Word came early the morning before Thanksgiving Day from the CAA that Ben had decided to come to Anchorage for the holiday. As soon as I got this information, I called the CAA in Bethel to try to get a message to tell him not to come to Anchorage because I was starting real labor. Tough luck, he had already boarded the plane for Anchorage. Borrowing Edna's car I went out to the airport to meet him.

When he got off of the plane, he was holding a suitcase in one hand, and in the other, Michele, a squirming toddler who looked like the most unkempt child in the world. Her beautiful long blond hair was a tangled mess, sticking out in tangles on one side and squashed in on the other like a bird's nest. Apparently, she had cried the first time Ben tried to brush her hair, therefore neither he nor any of her baby sitters attempted to brush it again.

It was three months since I had seen her and she had no idea who I was. She was a wild and totally undisciplined little one to whom I was a complete stranger. As he met me, Ben thrust her into my arms, leaving to make a phone call. Not wanting to look like a terrible mother, I first tried to calm her down, then made the major mistake of trying to brush her hair. Screams resulted. I gave up and just held her as gently as I could, with her sitting on my rather large abdomen. Feeling the glare of others in the waiting room. I was mortified.

After a while Ben returned and we went to a motel. A crib had been made available for Michele.

Ben left to see his friends at the NC company. I, fortunately had brought a couple of well-illustrated kid books with me and she warmed up to me as I read to her. After a few hours of reading she fell asleep. In the morning she told her daddy that I was the best baby sitter she had ever had.

By morning my labor pains were five minutes apart so Ben took Michele to Edna's, as we had previously arranged. On his return, he took me to Providence hospital where Dr. Peter Koeneger, the O B, and Dr. Helen Whaley, my pediatrician friend, were waiting. This was my only normal delivery. I was happy to have the competent care of these two. I do have to say that Renee arrived at the appropriate hour before lunch, so that we didn't have to bother my doctor friends too much. They were able to go home for their respective Thanksgiving dinners at the proper time. I really had to do this, because I had always tried to impress upon my own patients, that it was best to have their babies delivered during the day. Of course, this was selfish of me. I did love to be able to sleep at night.

In the meantime, poor Edna, who had volunteered for duty beyond any reason, took in Michele who, being dumped on another complete stranger, just howled until Edna had the bright idea of putting her in the bathtub. Michele loved being in the water and was happy as could be. Edna cooked and prepared Thanksgiving dinner for her guests, keeping a close eye on Michele. When dinnertime came, Michele refused to get out of the tub, screaming with Edna's every attempt. So, poor Edna gave her a turkey leg bone with a little meat on it to chew. There in the tub she remained until Ben came about 6 p.m. to reclaim her. Somehow I think I never really thanked Edna enough.

The nurses at Providence assured me that Renee was the most beautiful baby they had ever had in their delivery unit.

Five days later we were all back in Bethel, Michele happy with her new little baby sister, but that wasn't the end of adventures with the little ones.

154

In the middle of one night in Bethel when Renee was three weeks old, I woke up feeling chilled, so I went out to check on the children. I had put Renee in the well-padded easy chair in the front room so she wouldn't wake Michele up if she cried during the night.

There was a good reason for the cold I had felt. The front door had blown open and the wind was howling. The temperature was -30°F with a thirty mile an hour wind. Michele was fine in her little room, but Renee was so cold, she was absolutely blue. I took her into bed with me and slowly she warmed up with no after effects other than from then on she always seemed to love to be close to the warmest spot in any room.

Ben had decided that, as a foreigner from Holland, he would never go up the ladder of success unless he had a profession. He chose the law and after a series of tests from the Berkeley School of Law, taken under the supervision of the Bethel school principal, he was admitted to the Berkeley School of Law in California, with a very high grade. He was a bright man.

I hated to leave all my patients and friends and I definitely did not want to leave Alaska. After all my travels in my early years I knew that Alaska was my real home. I felt I had no other choice but to accede to my husband's wishes and I had hopes of returning to Alaska after Ben obtained his law degree.

We left Bethel in the latter part of November 1961, after four fascinating years. I loved the patients. The little girls giggled with a special Bethel giggle. It was melodious. But when we left I realized that I would not ever go back willingly to work in a place with such bleak weather in winter, with the cold blowing snow, and in summer with the 60°F mostly light drizzly rain, although I loved the people and to this day I miss them.

The Very Beginning

My parents met in the early 1920s in Ivy Depot, a tiny village in the mountains of Virginia. They fell in love and were married. My mother, Anna, was a social worker and my father an Episcopal missionary. Shortly after the marriage they heard a knock on their cabin door. A rather gruff and tough man from down the road stood there with, a little boy in tow.

"Here's George. You can have him."

The man, who had been out hunting, came home unexpectedly. He had a still in the corner of his house and spent most of his time making alcohol. He kept his rifle behind the door of his home, in case someone might report him to the Feds. George was five years old. He saw the rifle, picked it up and inadvertently pulled the trigger. There was a sudden blast and before his eyes his mother fell. When the man came home from hunting he found a wailing child and a dead wife. That was enough for him. He gave George to my parents.

Two years later my brother Stanford was born. It was such a terrible delivery that when my mother was close to term with me she went to Philadelphia where her parents lived.

I was born March 18, 1925, seventeen months later. She and I had great care in the Women's Hospital, but when my father came to see us, he took one look at me and said, "That is the ugliest baby I have ever seen." The nurses banished him.

After six weeks in the hospital we headed back to Ivy Depot, Virginia. My parents had unofficially adopted a couple of other kids. One was Alden Long. When my parents decided to go to Cuba as missionaries they had to make arrangement for them to live with friends to continue their schooling in the U.S.A. Thus, when I was two years old, the rest of us headed south. We flew first to Miami, then to Havana, Cuba.

From here we went to a small fishing village on the southernmost tip of Cuba. La Gloria was right on the water. There were no paved roads and my only memory of the trip is that of riding in an open wagon with all our belongings piled high beside us. A team of oxen drew the wagon. It had been raining heavily and the mud was knee

Mother and Jean, 1925

*Jean's mother's grandfather,
Alexander Williamson,
Philadelphia, PA. 1810(?)*

*Jean and Stan visiting
grandparents,
Philadelphia, PA, 1928*

*Women's Hospital in Philadelphia,
where Jean was born, 1925*

My first home, in Ivy Depot, Virginia, 1925

Jean and Stan on the rooftop of grandparents house in Philadelphia, 1930

Captain of the soccer team at St. Mary's boarding school, Peekskill, N.Y.

158

deep. Though we lurched and skidded from side to side, we never went off the road, thanks to a very skillful driver. After many uncomfortable wet hours, sitting on the bare uncovered boards of the wagon, we finally reached tiny La Gloria. Most of the scattered framed homes had thatched roofs, though some had corrugated tin roofs, making the homes exceptionally hot. Some were a good distance from the main dirt road. We came to a two-story clapboard house across the road from the church. It would be our home until the 1933 hurricane, six years later. The roads in the village were like footpaths, few wide enough for the wagons that would occasionally bring major supplies from the closest city. There was not a single car or other motorized vehicle in the village. The population was a mix of native Cubans, some English settlers and one Chinese family.

Our home was roomy and airy, whitewashed with a thatched roof. We found that this made the house much cooler than those with a tin roof. We also found that all sorts of bugs and other beasties, cockroaches, beetles, spiders, ants and even small snakes would drop down on us as we sat on the porch in the evenings. The downstairs revealed a short hallway that branched off to a good-sized living room housing our prized Atwater Kent radio. Despite all the static that marred the programs, the Atwater Kent was the only radio in town. Most of the people who came to Sunday evening service would gather here afterward to hear the news. If they were lucky, they could hear bits of news. The dining room on the right was more formal. The kitchen had a water pump, which we used whenever we needed water for drinking, bathing, cooking and general cleaning. The big event of the week was the required Saturday evening bath. Otherwise, washing was hit and miss. Stan and I preferred being dirty.

Our bedrooms were upstairs and we had an indoor bathroom having a bucket of water beside it to use for flushing. This was a luxury. On the wall of the steep back stairway there was a gas lamp that had to be carefully regulated. Once when it was turned up too high, the wall above it caught fire. This was scary but my father quickly doused the fire with a few buckets of water.

The house was built on stilts for flood protection. The stilts were not very high. Stan and I could easily wiggle our way under the house. Poppa could not. Stan was a bit of a firebug. One sunny day I helped him build a nice little fire under the house. Fortunately Poppa smelled the smoke and was able to reach it with a long pole. He was able to douse the fire with a bucket of water, then punished us severely. That was the end of our fire making, for a while.

Behind the house, enclosed by a high wire fence, was a small metal building. In the building my father mixed carbide with water to make acetylene, the gas that we used for the lamps in the house. Of course there was no electricity in La Gloria. The rest of the back yard had a big playhouse and a variety of trees, including orange, coconut, and lemon as well as guava bushes. Our mother used to pay the little Cuban boys five cents to shinny up the trees to knock down the ripe coconuts.

We were lucky to have Rosa, a nice maid who was in her twenties. I'm sure her pay was minimal but she was able to eat her meals with us. She cooked and helped keep the house in order. On Sundays, our regular dinner consisted always of chicken as the main dish, rice, and some vegetables. Rosa would first catch one of our many chickens, wring its neck, place it on a flat tree stump, then chop off its head. The body would flop around for several minutes. Stan and I could not eat our chickens. Mostly we ate the rice. As a result both of us stayed skinny.

The tall, narrow church was less than a block from our house. Poppa was so proud of the Spanish that he had been studying ever so diligently, that he tried to use it at his first service. Announcing the time of the next mass, he stated in his new language that the crow would cackle at eight o'clock. The Cubans dissolved in laughter. He never lived that down.

We had a Chinese laundryman. Once a week he would come to the house, and go through the rooms to pick up all the dirty clothes from baskets. He took them away and the next week would bring them back, put them away in their proper drawers, again picking up a new supply of dirty clothes to launder.

Stan and I were not big advocates of church going. Every Sunday morning we managed to be the last of the family, all washed and dressed in our Sunday best, to leave the house. We took care to only partially close the garden gate latch. No sooner than we were seated in the second pew of the church with our mother, than our little dog

Pedro, would come running up the aisle with his tail wagging, looking for us. Needless to say it took both Stan and me to catch him, then to carry him back home very slowly and return to church even more slowly. For some reason our mother never seemed to mind our misbehavior and all was forgiven or forgotten by the time we got home for dinner, until the next Sunday.

Poppa was a slender man, about five-foot-ten, with mostly white hair, though he was only thirty-seven when we reached Cuba. Our mother was almost as tall as he and though not overweight, certainly weighed more than he. Both were good and special people but they did not get along well and argued frequently. Stan and I decided never to marry anyone with whom we would argue as they did. Poppa was a little distant, busy with his work, while our mother was warm and loving. A piece of chocolate cake was always handy if one of us fell and scratched a knee.

What was the source of income for the small village? I have no idea. All the men fished. We were never without a supply of fish. But there was no grocery store, no post office, no industry that I can recall, no newspaper, no doctor or dentist. We ordered whatever we needed from Havana. The supplies arrived by wagon as we ourselves had come.

Our mother was the disciplinarian. When she caught us being naughty, she paddled us with her wood-backed hairbrush. My brother was smart. He howled loud and long the first time he was paddled. Not wanting the neighbors to think she was mistreating him she gave him minimal punishment. On the other hand I was stubborn and refused to utter a sound, thus getting paddled much harder and much longer but giving no satisfaction to my poor mother.

Stan and I had many Cuban playmates. Nothing pleased us more than to be mistaken for a Cuban with our tans. Mother taught us by the Calvert School system. We sat at regular desks in the front yard in the shade of the trees. When we did return to the USA, I joined the fourth grade at eight years of age. Stan was in the fifth grade. We hated to be confined in a schoolroom.

For fun after a rain, Stan and I loved to go barefoot in the muddy road. There was nothing that could compare to the squishy, squashy mud under foot, oozing out between our toes. There was a bad result from this pleasure, however. We became riddled with parasites. The worst of these was the hookworm that caused us both to become severely anemic. On our return to the USA years later, we spent months going to the doctor taking one medicine after another to get rid of these unwelcome invaders. But that mud was fun.

When Poppa got mad at me, I would run to my favorite tree, and like my friends, shinny up high above his reach, then work my way out on one of the stronger branches to hang upside down by my legs. Poor Poppa, he would get so angry and so frustrated, but by the time I would come down his anger would have subsided.

When I was seven, we had a class-five hurricane, though at that time we didn't know about the grades given to hurricanes. Poppa heard about it on the radio and went out to warn the villagers, telling them to get to shelter quickly. We went across the road to a one-story well-built brick cottage owned by an English lady. It was much stronger than our flimsy wood house. At least thirty-two people were crowded in together. The wind and rain started slowly, then increased to become a ferocious storm. The corrugated-tin roofs of some of the buildings were whipped off, flying through the air slicing through any object in their path. Unfortunately some of the objects were human. Most of us in the house did not think we would survive. Our own house was lifted high in the air and came crashing down into pieces that were quickly blown away. The church was next to go flying by. Later, the only things we found were the silver candlesticks and the crucifix. On the porch of the cottage we gathered closely together and we all sang, "Nearer My God to Thee."

The winds slowly subsided. Most everyone rushed out, happy to be alive, searching for survivors, thinking the storm was over. Again Poppa went out to warn everyone that this was the quiet center of the storm and that the worst part was yet to come. He took with him as many men as he could find to help. The people had to know that the storm would return and would be much worse. Some did not believe the news. Of those who did not seek shelter, many lost limbs or were killed.

During the second part of the storm, my mother held on to me tightly because I was crying—not because I was afraid, but because I had seen our maid Rosa's house blow away. Rosa was with us, but my new sailor suit was in her house. My mother consoled me. Grandmother would get me a new one. My grandmother never did.

After the storm was finally over, the men went out to look for survivors. They carried back a man with a badly mangled leg. Somehow a doctor reached our village the next day. He amputated the leg in the house and the leg was buried in the back yard. The next day our dog, Pedro, dug it up.

The Red Cross sent supplies by wagon, arriving a few days later. People were getting very hungry. Poppa was in charge of giving out food and clothing. It was an orderly distribution with grateful recipients. However, along came a man who was from Jamaica. He was a Seventh Day Adventist and could eat no pork. Poppa didn't realize it but the cans of beans he gave him had pork in them. The man was infuriated, pulled a knife and tried to slash Poppa. Stan got into the fray, ending up with a cut, but then some of the men subdued the man and Cuba deported him home to Jamaica.

With no church left, the men of the village put up poles with a thatched roof stretched over the top of the poles for church. It was fine except for rainy days. To celebrate the survivors, there was a big picnic on the following Fourth of July. Early in the day, some of the men dug a big hole in the ground, making a wood fire in the hole that burned down slowly to make very hot coals. Then they killed a pig, disemboweled it in front of all the kids watching and ran a pole through it. They placed the pole with the pig on forked poles at each end of the fire hole. We all took turns roasting the pig over the coals, a process that took hours and hours. After the roasting was complete, everyone had a great feast: pig, corn, and watermelon. It was a happy day. I've never forgotten it.

It was now July of 1933 and I was eight years old. With no home and no real church for Poppa, we headed north. Poppa, not the best of drivers, had gotten a Model T Ford on one of his trips to Havana to see the Bishop. In fact, he had never driven before he got this car. Not too long into his drive home from Havana to La Gloria, he skidded off the road and rolled over a few times. Fortunately some men came along in a wagon and pulled him out of the car. He had a long gash in his leg, but they were able to stop the bleeding. The men got the car back on the road so he could continue his drive home. He ended up with a ten-inch scar on his right leg, but had no other residual from his accident.

At any rate the car still functioned. We had few possessions to pack, mostly food supplies with enough water to last till we reached Camaguey, our destination. This was a long and arduous journey in our Model T. We followed the lonely, narrow dirt road with high cliffs on our left side with many caves in the cliffs. Bandits were known to hide in the caves and Stan and I spent much of our time looking at the caves hoping to see some sign of the bandits. We never saw another vehicle during the whole trip. Between the cliffs and the road were masses of brush. On the right side of the road was a beautiful forest filled with birds.

The next part of our trip was really scary for us all. The air suddenly became filled with smoke and soon there was so much smoke we could barely see. Then on our right side, we saw huge flames shooting up into the sky. To breathe we held wet towels over our faces. Then the flames leapt across the road just ahead of us and all the brush caught fire. Poppa had to make an instant decision, which he did, gunning the car, probably all the way up to thirty miles an hour, and went right through the fire. How Poppa made it and still remained on that road remains a mystery. It had been a hot day before but with the heat from the fire we were almost roasting, literally.

By nightfall we reached Camaguey—a regular city, where Poppa became an assistant to the clergyman at St. Paul's. Stan and I went to the church school, our first formal school. All classes were in Spanish, but we were fluent by then. The school uniform consisted of white shirts with a red tie, with blue skirts for the girls and blue pants for the boys. One of my classmates' names was Castro.

After the school session was over, we went north, this time to Havana by train. No sooner had the train started when the station behind us exploded. The Cuban revolution of 1933 had begun. We stayed in Havana for a few months, but then our father decided that things were too dangerous for us to stay longer so he arranged to get us flown to Miami. He stayed behind to work with the ABC, the underground. Mother, Stan, and I made a safe journey to Miami. The next plane from Havana to Miami was shot down. As an East Indian once said to me, after a bad accident in Africa, "Your time has not yet come." Indeed it had not.

At least a year later, we went to meet my father at the train station in Philadelphia, where we were living with our grandparents. Poppa had filled letters to my mother with stories of bullets flying overhead in the second story building where he was living. When he got off the train, he was almost unrecognizable: skinny, leaning forward on a cane like a very old man. It took months for him to recuperate from his adventures in Cuba.

Jean and Stan at school in Cuba—taught by Mother,
Rosa helping Stan, 1931

Mother, Stan, and Jean posing with the pilot in Miami,
returning to the USA.

After landing in the village of Rampart, husband Bob Whaley took this picture on his Comanche airplane. Michele, Renee, Jean, and Tammy.

Bob and Jean get married at home by brother Stan and sister-in-law, Elaine—May 29, 1976

Jean and Bob in Munich, Germany, at dinner, 1986

RECENT DAYS

*Bob and Jean motorcycling in
Austria, 1985*

*Motorcycling in the
Swiss Alps, 1987*

*Jean and Bob riding on an elephant in Thailand
where they went for William and Mimi Fraser's wedding, 1999*

RECENT DAYS

Jean in front of her home in Anchorage, 1995

Jean at home in Anchorage with Suzie and Sheba, 1999

Jean and Bob on the Alaska ferry, 2002

WHO WILL ROCK THE CRADLE
WHEN I'M GONE?

When I am gone, and I don't plan to be gone for many years, I will have some formidable replacements.

First is the teacher, Michele, an exceptional individual. Her students are her primary focus, taking much more time than they should; yet she is so full of enthusiasm that she generates the same in her classes. The extra curricular work she does is found in many good teachers, but she always does the above-and-beyond activities that help her students to excel. Her own two daughters work with her as well, playing music, skiing, running, and other sports and also doing a variety of creative artwork.

The second, Renee, is one of strong character, a mother of three, loyal and determined to do the best she can for her family. Two daughters and a son are being raised with great care and they know they are loved, yet they know their boundaries. She is involved in all their school activities and all their sports, of which there are many. She, like her sister above, is a workaholic—rarely stopping to rest.

Then there is the youngest, Tammy, a registered nurse who has worked in Intensive Care, and now in the Emergency Room, which she finds even more of a challenge. In her first work most of the patients were too ill or comatose, but now she has to deal with patients who can move about, ask questions, some of whom resist orders and may become violent and dangerous. However she is warm and caring, efficient and capable, and so is able to cope well.

My brother, Stan, who died over ten years ago courtesy of a too-early Medicare discharge, was the most unselfish person I have ever known. Now I find his characteristics have been instilled in my three offspring.

For these three I am deeply grateful; I know that when my time does come I will have no fear about who will rock the cradle for all those they hold dear.

Appendix A

Tuberculosis—The Scourge of Alaska

Tuberculosis is a bacterial disease with an unusual type of bacteria, which is slow growing and persistent. Primarily a disease of the lungs, it is spread easily throughout the body via the lymphatics and the blood. Because of its sedentary nature, the bacterial disease may have a slow and insidious progression that causes cavitary lesions in the lungs and abscesses in many other tissues. These include the liver, the kidneys, ovaries, intestines, bladder, and brain. Plaques may form in the liver and in the brain, where, because of pressure by the plaques, seizures may occur. Tuberculosis meningitis was common, because of the infection.

In discussing tuberculosis with the noted pulmonary specialist, Dr. Robert Fraser, who ran the Alaska State Program for Case Finding of tuberculosis in the state, he gave me a good bit of information: by 1955, 55 percent of children entering school were tuberculin positive, and by third grade 70 percent were positive. He believes that the introduction of tuberculosis in the early 1930s, probably brought by the white man, acted like a new disease in communities with low resistance. With increased communication between the villages by dog sled in the winter and boat in the summer, tuberculosis was rampant in the early 1940s and 1950s.

The death rate from the disease was high and there was little treatment that could be offered, unless the patients were in a hospital bed in one of the small regional Alaska Native Service hospitals in Mt. Edgecomb, in a sanatorium in Washington State, or later in the Anchorage Native hospital.

The hospital treatment consisted of rest and good food, although, unless the food was Native, the patients were not happy with it. One of the medications available for tuberculosis was paraminosalicylic acid (PAS), a horrible yellow grittty substance mixed with water or juice. PAS had to be taken three or four times a day. The patients hated it.

The only other medications at that time were injections of Streptomycin and Dihydrostreptomycin, and the latter caused deafness. The death rate from the disease was high.

170

Dr. Fraser worked closely with the state Public Health nurses. Together, they covered the villages in Alaska.

Although some scientists found the tuberculosis bacteria in two thousand-year-old bones found in the Barrow area, other scientists believed that tuberculosis was brought to Alaska by the early Europeans. Because of the distance between the villages, and very little contact with one another, the early tuberculosis disease was confined to the village affected.

The Arctic Health Research, a branch of the Center for Disease Control (CDC), under the direction of Dr. George Comstock began studies with Isoniazid (INH) in the villages in 1954. The first studies were undertaken in my Tanana villages. My staff nurse, Birgit Dahlstrom, became the nurse who dispensed the INH pills and placebos to the villagers. Later, when I was in Bethel, Alaska, studies with INH were being done.

Results from the tests showed that INH not only prevented tuberculosis, but also, was able to cure the disease in many patients. This was a great step forward in the control of tuberculosis.

Later, X-ray surveillance teams were sent out by the Public Health Department to the villages to keep tabs on the course of tuberculosis. Because of the significant chance of recurrence of tuberculosis in those villagers who had been treated, some were found who needed to be retreated.

By 1973, most of the hospital beds for tuberculosis had been closed. The disease was considered controlled. However, at this current time, tuberculosis is still a significant disease in Alaska, showing resurgence because of the number of patients who did not complete their therapy.

The development of resistance is a natural evolution of bacteria, but added to, by the many cases of partial treatment of the disease, the tuberculosis bacteria has become resistant to the medication. Now, infected individuals may have to take three and four medications for a longer period, under close supervision by the Public Health nurses or the local village medical aids.

In recent years, the development of HIV infections has resulted in the destruction of the human body immune defense to other diseases, including tuberculosis. This has increased the number of tuberculosis cases, and most all HIV patients are now tested for tuberculosis, many of whom are now being treated for both diseases.

ORDER FORM

I would like to order my own or another copy of the book *Alaskan Adventures in Medicine* by Jean Persons, M.D. Please send me:

\# books x \$16.95 per copy =

+ Postage (first class) & Handling @ \$4.95/book: _____

TOTAL ENCLOSED   \$

_____

We accept cash, check, or money order made out to Northbooks, or VISA, Mastercard. Prices subject to change without notice.

(You may phone your VISA/MC order to Northbooks at 907-696-8973)

VISA/MC card # ⬜⬜⬜⬜ ⬜⬜⬜⬜ ⬜⬜⬜⬜ ⬜⬜⬜⬜

Exp. Date: ___ / ___   Amount Charged: \$ _____

Signature: _____

Phone Number: _____

Please send my book (s) to:

Name: _____

Address: _____

City: _____ State: _____ Zip: _____

Fill out this order form and send to:

ΠORTHBOOKS
17050 N. Eagle River Loop Rd, #3
Eagle River, AK 99577-7804
(907) 696-8973
www.northbooks.com

CPSIA information can be obtained
at www.ICGtesting.com
Printed in the USA
FFOW05n2320170314

9 780978 976620